A BOOK OF FAMILY PRAYER

A BOOK of FAMILY PRAYER

Gabe Huck

The Seabury Press / New York

For all the saints, but especially
for my father and for Joseph Caulfield
and for Gerald Ecker: they pray
for me in different ways.

First Paperback Printing

1983 · The Seabury Press
815 Second Avenue · New York, N.Y. 10017

Library of Congress Cataloging in Publication Data

Huck, Gabe.   A book of family prayer.
1. Family—Prayer-books and devotions—English. I. Title.
BX2170.F3H82   242'.8   78-26651   ISBN: 0-8164-2486-1

ACKNOWLEDGMENTS

Grateful acknowledgment is made to the following people and institutions for permission to use the materials listed:

CENTRAL CONFERENCE OF AMERICAN RABBIS: the following texts from *Gates of Prayer*, copyright by the Central Conference of American Rabbis: "Let all rejoice with all their might" from "O Holy Sabbath Day"; "At this hour of memorial we recall"; and "Blessed is the match" by Hannah Senesch. The following texts from the Passover meal are taken from *A Passover Haggadah*, copyright by the Central Conference of American Rabbis and used by permission: "Now in the presence of loved ones"; "You have called us for service"; "Among people everywhere, sharing of bread"; "This is the bread of affliction"; "We were slaves to Pharaoh in Egypt"; "He went down to Egypt with meager numbers"; "When the Egyptian armies were drowning in the sea"; the various replies to the questions: "What is the meaning of. . ."; "In every generation"; "Friends, let us say Grace"; "May He who blessed Abraham"; "The injustice of this world"; "May the All Merciful."

THE CHURCH HYMNAL CORPORATION: "O Lord of all, with us abide," from "Joy dawned again on Easter Day," copyright by The Church Pension Fund. Used by Permission.

CONCORDIA PUBLISHING HOUSE: text of hymn "Thy Strong Word Did Cleave the Darkness" by Martin Franzman, from *The Worship Supplement*, © 1969 by Concordia Publishing House. Reprinted by permission.

CONFRATERNITY OF CHRISTIAN DOCTRINE: Scripture texts used in this work are taken from the *New American Bible*, copyright © 1970 by the Confraternity of Christian Doctrine, Washington, D.C., and are used by license of said copyright owner. No part of the *New American Bible* may be reproduced in any form without permission in writing from the copyright owner. All rights reserved.

FARRAR, STRAUS & GIROUX, INC.: "O the chimneys," excerpted with the permission of Farrar, Straus & Giroux, Inc., from *O the Chimneys* by Nelly Sachs, translated from the German by Michael Roloff, copyright © 1967 by Farrar, Straus & Giroux, Inc.

GREGORIAN INSTITUTE OF AMERICA, INC.: "Careworn Mother Stood Attending," translation by Edward McKenna, from *Worship II*, © 1975, GIA Publications.

CONTENTS

FOREWORD

The finger points to the moon.
Woe to the one who mistakes the finger for the moon.
A ZEN KOAN.

To have a book for family prayer is not yet to have a praying family. The two are readily distinguishable. But this book is a pointer to a traditional path. It offers a way for a household to begin a common journey.

The path proposed here is genuinely conservative; it is also creative. It reflects the sensitivity of someone whose own life has been touched by a living tradition and who wants to make that tradition more accessible to others.

The tradition in question is the tradition of Christian liturgical prayer. It is not the liturgy of the churches and the monasteries, however. Rather, this volume sets out the materials for a domestic liturgy—the liturgy of the Christian household.

That form of liturgy is undoubtedly less familiar than the liturgies of the public assemblies of the churches. Nevertheless, domestic liturgy incorporates characteristic features of all liturgical prayer: (1) the *assembling* of the household at recurring intervals of some regularity; (2) marking *moments of time*—hours, days, weeks, seasons, occasions—as suitable for celebrating the elusive presence of a saving God; (3) *ordering the household assembly* so that the one who leads promotes the participation of the whole assembly in appropriate ways; (4) public reading from the books of Scripture on a designated schedule; (5) *using patterned gestures and words* that promote ease in prayer through their familiarity and engender surprise through their symbolic power; and (6) *promoting personal prayerfulness* beyond the common prayer of the liturgical assembly.

The domestic liturgy, like the liturgy of church and monastery, is not intended to exhaust the prayer of the people who come together. Nor does liturgical prayer substitute for personal prayerfulness. On the contrary, corporate prayer expresses living faith, and in expressing it intensifies it. It begins and ends in prayer.

Moreover, just as *A Book of Family Prayer* is not intended to replace personal piety but to strengthen it, the book does not intend to substitute household prayer for the public worship of the church. It aims to promote a mutually beneficial relationship between them. What is done in one assembly, either public or domestic, is enriched by what occurs in the other.

The appearance of *A Book of Family Prayer* at this time is significant, for the publication may mark a turning point in the reappropriation of a tradition almost lost to a full generation. People who led the way in the liturgical movement of the 1940's and 50's encouraged regular corporate prayer in families as an important expression of the movement among lay Christians. When the popular movement culminated in official liturgical reforms in the decades of the 60's and 70's, a curious disruption set in. The practice of prayer at home declined. A convergence of factors, only a few of them ecclesiastical, made traditional piety suspect. But many of the pious and devout of a new generation, confused and led to expect little help from the churches, turned eastward or inward or to the just-developing charismatic movement for help in the way of prayer. Some lost heart and also their interest in praying altogether.

When Gabe Huck approached The Liturgical Conference in 1977 with a proposal for *A Book of Family Prayer*, Bob Hovda, then editor of Conference programs and publications, recognized the timeliness of the proposal and recommended it to the executive committee of the Conference board of directors. All of us knew that Huck was eminently qualified to undertake the project. He, too, had been a Conference writer and editor of the Conference's membership journal, *Liturgy*. More importantly, he and his own family had maintained the practice of daily household prayer throughout a troublesome decade.

So convinced were we, in fact, of the importance of the project that The Liturgical Conference, a 40-year-old association concerned with promoting liturgical renewal, turned to Seabury, a major publisher with the capacity to reach the general religious public who would want to know about the availability of *A Book of Family Prayer*. Those conversations have culminated in this publication.

To have a book for family prayer is not yet to have a praying family, any more than simple purchase of a bible makes a household Christian. But this book, and a bible, opened within the household daily offer people who share roof, table, bed, a creative way to enter into a living tradition and to continue on a common journey.

MARY COLLINS, O.S.B.
President, The Liturgical Conference
Washington, D.C.

PRAYER AT HOME
An Introduction

Alone and Together

We pray. We fumble for expressions of ourselves toward God. Our prayer is a word, a gesture, a silence, a cry or a roar or a whisper. Our prayer is not found in books but in our hearts. Books can only recognize some of the times and ways our tradition gives us, can reflect upon these in the special difficulties of the present generation and then offer a little help.

What is strong in our tradition, and in that of most religions, is a rhythm of prayer flowing through each day, defining each week, creating the seasons of the year. To pray on awakening, with meals, at bedtime; to keep our Sabbath holy with special prayer; to live in Lent or Eastertime and to mark the great festivals: this book hopes only to give these traditions some chance to breathe life into our homes. Most of what is included here, as well as its basic arrangement, is drawn from Christian tradition with the full recognition that the dominant sources of that tradition are Jewish.

There are difficulties: pressures, schedules, demands and preoccupations that make it hard to have a space in our mind or in our world for regular praying. A book cannot create that space, only suggest some of the ways it is worth creating. To live in faith demands a habit of prayer that is too important to be left to the church building or to professional religious or to an hour on Sunday. Prayer is the rest that gives sense and rhythm and beauty to all our movement. It is the art of every Christian.

The prayers of this book are meant to be useful whether one lives alone or with others. Some of the prayers are for use by an individual even in a family setting. But most can be used by several persons praying together. Often the word *family* or *household* is used, but this usually means many things besides mother, father and children; it can mean single-parent families, older couples, young couples without children, single persons or even a person alone. It is in all such basic units that Christian life needs expression in prayer.

When persons live together and when there is a sharing of belief, of what things mean, of what is hoped for, of what is important, then there can be prayer, there needs to be prayer. That is our tradition: "Where two or three are gathered in my name, there am I in their midst" (Mt. 18:20). Prayer is the ordinary doing of ordinary people. Alone or with others, it is shaped by us and shapes us. It speaks what we have in common with all who have responded to the one God, touching those deepest parts of our selves that we share across ages no matter what the shape of our cities and sciences.

Learning to Pray

Young or old, we learn to pray by praying. We come to be at home with prayer. And home is what and where prayer must be. If prayer is to be familiar ground, a place where we are comfortable, then prayer needs to flow through life where it is lived.

More than the accepted doctrines of the faith or the codes of morality, it is how we pray that forms us in faith. The prayer at home and in community gives shape to everything else, makes the teachings and the morality and the church structures personal, makes them a part of the one praying.

The church's constant prayer is eucharistic, the giving of great things to the Lord. But that is not something that happens apart from people. It is people who give thanks, people who are eucharistic. That thanksgiving happens when the Sunday eucharist simply expresses what happens all the time: the giving thanks to God that fills sleeping, waking, eating, working, loving.

All our prayer is born in wonder at God's presence. As always, such presence is recognized in simple and humble ways: our enjoyment of the presence of other persons, our deeds of compassion to those who suffer, the way we savor the joys of seeing and smelling, even our pain and our frustration. Out of this simple wonder comes our prayer. Prayer is not an "ought to," it is a response, an answer. Its vocabulary is filled with silence, folded hands, burning candles, kneeling, breaking bread. Words are only one part of responding to the wonder of God's presence and sometimes they are not needed at all.

Children learn to pray from parents and other adults who live in God's presence and who respond with prayer. They learn to pray, not because parents feel that they ought to pray for the child's sake, but because parents have a love of praying and a habit of praying for their own sake. Ideally, the child comes into a home where prayer is already important. Or as the child grows up the parents are discovering prayer and the child can take part in that discovery.

Sometimes the presence of children will mean shaping the prayer in special ways so that they can take part. But there are limits to this, the danger that prayer can be turned into something childish, something to grow out of. Most often, a good prayer will be good for adults and children, although one may enter into it far more deeply than another. The Lord's Prayer, a short psalm, joining hands at table, singing to welcome the coming of the Sabbath, can all be good prayers at any age, for the feelings and meanings which they carry are timeless.

Scattered throughout this book are prayers and thoughts especially appropriate to children. For the most part, however, the various prayers can be used by adults alone or by adults and children. Adults should always avoid using prayer to display how cute or how intelligent a child is. Prayer can certainly take on a variety of moods, playful or delightful, but it is never to be a show by child or by adult. Nor is it to be drudgery, a demand, or a bore. It cannot be these things if it is really a response to the presence of God and if adults know something of the riches of Christian prayer and the rhythm of days and seasons.

If prayer is a habit in the home, then there will not be a

question of how old a child should be before beginning to pray. The child will naturally be present at times when the parents pray, and little by little will become part of the prayer. As the child grows, the parents can watch for the opportunity to give the child parts in the prayer that he or she can do well.

And what of times when an older child does not want to be present for prayer? Much depends on the family. Little is gained from forcing attendance. Parents who know their own need to pray together will not be threatened by a child's need to remain apart on occasion. Much also depends on what prayer it is. If the family normally joins in the blessing and thanksgiving before a meal, then it would seem normal that all who are to share at table be present for the blessing. Adults who strive to live in a world filled with the awe of God's presence should know best of all just how difficult it can be on some days and at some stages in life to have any sense of this at all; to force common prayer at such times ignores the delicate life of prayer itself.

It is said that religion is not taught but caught. Now praying together is not religion and teaching prayers is not teaching religion. Religion is the way one loves, works, eats, gives, takes, does justice. Prayer is the way people have of gathering up their whole lives and what those lives mean to them. Such prayer is a habit, the stuff of every morning, night and meal. It is also the stuff of unique moments, special joys or angers or fears or sorrows.

The prayers of this book are, for the most part, the everyday prayers. They are the prayers of habit rather than prayers for times of special need. To be a part of any family, they need this everydayness. A family may use only a few to begin with and be committed to them, or to whatever variation seems to work for them. Many prayers are included here, but in most cases that is only to broaden the choices, not to give an "all or nothing" feeling. Prayerbooks have nearly always been used this way in our tradition.

Few of us today have grown up rich in the vocabulary of our prayer traditions. We tend to feel that we have little for ourselves and less to pass on to our children. In a way, we too have to learn all the words and the rhythms of prayer that have served our ancestors whose times were no less difficult than our own. In our twenties or our sixties we can discover that praying together is not something for the few, but rather the task and the art and the joy of the ordinary Christian. It does not mean setting oneself apart, claiming any unique vocation or experience. It means only expressing the thanksgiving that is in spite of everything, because of everything.

The Time of Prayer

This, then, is not really a book *of* prayers, but a book *for* prayer. It is incomplete without an individual or group and then it is but a tool, a help. There are prayers for the morning and evening, for meals, for the weekdays and Sundays of the special seasons and the ordinary times. These are the prayer times of habit, like the Angelus. They do not come because, on a particular day, we are happy or sad or in trouble, but they come with the very moments themselves, the little turning points of each day when life itself nudges us to give thanks. They are brought on by nothing but habits in our lives. So, if the book is to serve its purpose, it must be there every morning at bedside or every evening on the table—till perhaps it is no longer needed.

Daily prayer, especially when done by two or more together, needs a firm commitment to a time when it will rarely have to be missed. For some that is the morning, for some the mealtime, for some the night. And when someone is gone, the one or ones left pray.

The length of the prayer depends on what feels comfortable. Most of the prayers in this book, even with a minute of silence, take less than five minutes without a scripture reading. The pace of the prayer is more important than the length. Better fewer prayers without rushing, savoring the silent times, feeling quiet and easy and at home in the prayer. Saint Benedict said it well fifteen centuries ago: "Our prayer ought to be short and pure, unless it happens to be prolonged by an inspiration of divine grace. In community, however, let prayer be very short . . ."

Pace and length of these prayers depend somehow on how

much can be known "by heart," which is where our prayer
starts. Sometimes being able to read doesn't help, even works
against us. Thus today we often know very few prayers by heart,
but we hear or read a multitude of prayers through the Sunday
liturgy. The prayer forms here intend that prayer by heart become a greater part of daily prayer. Memorizing prayers simply
frees us from the page; where we go from there depends
somewhat on keeping an easy pace in prayer, even when simply
breathing a morning prayer while dressing. The words are free
to encircle our whole selves.

The Cycle of Prayer

There are moods to our days, and so there are moods to the
days of the church. From ancient traditions with many roots
older than Christianity, such days have been gathered as seasons and named Advent, Christmastime, Lent, Eastertime. Each
has its own feeling, each tells its own story, each has its colors
and textures and smells. They are like various rooms in a
grandmother's long-lived-in house. Their feelings reflect our
feelings. Their stories—of waiting or birth or dying or rising—
are our story. Through the flow of the year with these seasons
and with the feasts and the ordinary weeks and days, we circle
round who I am, who we are as family and as church. Year by
year, each season brings its songs, its foods, its colors, its words.
They are the same, familiar and friendly, yet new because we
are not the same voices, lips, eyes, mouth. We have grown a bit.

For Advent, Christmastime, Lent and Eastertime, this book
offers special daily and Sunday prayers for the morning and
evening. Each season also has a number of prayers and sometimes various customs for its own unique days. The calendar of
the years with the dates of their seasons and the calendar of the
months with the dates of various feasts should guide the user to
each week's prayers.

Our times are also marked by days that recall people and
events. Saints' days—anniversaries of the deaths of men and
women who lived here long ago or just last year—do this. Their
presence and their communion with all of us is something to

celebrate. To some extent, we must name our own saints so that the calendar we finally follow has names from every different gathering of the church: this individual household, the neighborhood, the local church, the region, the universal church. These days keep us in touch; they keep things human by telling the saint's human stories; they root us in times and places where the people and problems may not look so different from here and now.

Through all the weeks of seasons and of ordinary time we have another rhythm in our lives. That is the rhythm of the week and the Sabbath. Times change, work weeks and leisure times shift, but God's gift of Sabbath, our Sunday, must somehow remain. Sunday is the sacrament of creation and of redemption, and keeping it holy is a way to live in the presence of these mysteries. The prayer of Sunday is unique. It welcomes the arrival of the Lord's Day, of the Lord present in the day. It blesses our time of restoration and renewal. It gathers us for eucharist. Finally, the prayer of Sunday separates this day from the rest of the week. Even during the seasons Sunday retains its own identity. Vatican Council II called Sunday "the original feast day" and "a day of joy." The prayers provided for Sunday, drawn largely from Jewish prayers for the Sabbath, change only slightly with the seasons. They are meant to accompany whatever efforts a group makes to keep Sunday special.

There is yet another rhythm in our lives—that of life itself: conceiving, giving birth, nourishing, washing, caring, growing to maturity, parting, choosing, hurting, reconciling, healing, dying. These are turning points in every human story. At a home, a little gathering of the church, we may mark these moments with prayers in which we marvel at what has happened. In the larger church, the congregation, we also know the moments that surround and mark the initiation of a new Christian in baptism, confirmation and eucharist; we know the caring for the sick and its prayer; we know the gradual work of healing and forgiving; we know the commitment to marriage and the commitment to ministry. All these are so common to the church, yet each is unique for it is happening to this person and this congregation right now.

The Place for Prayer

The main thing to be said here is not that this place or that is better for praying, but that most of us will be more faithful to our prayer if there is a place in the home where that prayer regularly happens. Just as we consider the rhythm of everyday life in the home when agreeing to keep a regular time for prayer in the morning, at night, or at meals, so we look to where we are at that time, or where we could be. Two places deserve special attention: the table and the bedside are very human places to gather and pray.

The table is our gathering: we never stay away for long. We get hungry. The table brings us face to face, sharing food and talk and self, as close to being equals as we ever get. The table is the possible occasion to delight in food and in fellowship. We slow down. We stop. We are needed by each other. We serve each other. The meal of the home embodies what we profess to mean about living together: we mean life to each other, we mean delight to each other. So the table is the natural place to express life and delight, to make some gesture for the thanks to God that we mean by being Christian.

The bed is the place of rest, renewal, lovemaking, birth, fear of the dark, dreaming, nightmares, pain, anticipation, weakness, peacemaking, death. Our prayer of morning and of night are never far from such moments and, alone or together, they would be at home beside the bed, kneeling or standing. The private prayers of early morning and of night which are given in this book almost presume the marvelous presence of the bed.

Prayer at home, by table or bed, can keep us in touch with what living is all about. Those two pieces of life's furniture are constant contact with what is so common, so simple and so constant.

But sometimes, especially during the days of Advent or Lent, we may create a special place of prayer. This could be the space where the advent wreath stands, or the space in front of the lenten cross, or the table where a bowl of ashes reminds us of the struggle from winter to spring that Lent is all about. Eastertime may call for a place of prayer outdoors where resurrection proclaims itself from garden or blossoming tree or new flowers in a window box. What is important about such special places is consistency and simplicity. Most often it is enough that there be a single visual focus: the cross or a candle, the Christmas tree, a branch, a flower.

The Stuff of Prayer

Words are not the prayers. Praying together, even when it is only for a minute, is something that limits words. Words go only so far when they must help us do something as delightful and weighty as praying. So in prayer we call on other ways we humans have of expressing ourselves individually and as communities.

Praying together is not so easy today. The times have not encouraged us in such non-word ways of self-expression. Such things as music and singing are left to professionals today. Silence is often considered abnormal and makes us uneasy. Printed matter and the electronic media have multiplied the reading and hearing of words till we can scarcely judge a string of words that are beautifully put together from the fine print of an insurance policy.

Deciding to pray forces some confrontations with such ways of living. For prayer has always depended on caring about words, on not being afraid to let song and music of all kinds put movement and rhythm to voice and body, on fashioning or finding something beautiful made by human hands from God's gifts to be the candle or the bread, on not worrying about a silence taking hold and doing its work. Now no one can take all that on at once. We need to begin slowly, getting used to the pace and the stuff of praying together, getting used to thinking about prayer together as more than words.

Sounds and Silences

Nearly every prayer in this book suggests at some point that there be song, at some point that there be silence. Usually the songs are familiar or can be sung to familiar tunes. But singing religious songs—or any songs at all—at home is not that comfortable for most of us. Not at the start. We may be tempted to skip the song. Or to simply read it, thus making it another spoken prayer. That would be missing the whole dimension which music gives to prayer, and that dimension is sound: the ups and downs, longs and shorts, louds and softs. A song is not just its words. A song is fast or slow, it is loud or soft, it is marching or lamenting or rejoicing. The qualities of a song can create the sound of Advent or Lent, just as certain carols can make the sound of Christmas or certain rhythms and instruments can make the sound of a parade.

Everyone knows how a tune can enter into a person and, at the right moment, spring up in whistling or humming or singing. That seems natural. Our song at prayer has this same naturalness. In fact, humming or whistling would occasionally be appropriate as would the use of piano, guitar, flute, violin or any instrument that a member of the household can play. Sometimes the words can be left out altogether, letting the sound do the work all alone.

Music, here in prayer, is just that: prayer. If it is to be prayer, then we have to be at ease with it, doing the best we can, not worrying about what anyone will think. Parents, praying with children, need to sing unself-consciously, not checking always to see if the child has joined in. Humans have always found that raising their voices to get the full variety of sounds has been inseparable from prayer. Somehow it touches our soul in a way that simple speech cannot.

Some may be surprised that simple well-known tunes have been suggested in this book to be used with the words of various religious hymns and psalms. Hopefully the mood of the tune fits the time of day or year for which it is suggested. There is nothing new in this borrowing of tunes from folk or popular music; the church has always felt quite free to take the tunes that people know and like and to fill them with special words. Families familiar with other songs from Sunday worship should feel free to substitute these whenever appropriate.

Silence is every bit as important as sound. Throughout these prayers, usually following a psalm or a scripture reading, silence is suggested. But silence also takes some getting used to. How

long an individual or a group keeps silent depends on the over-
all length of the prayer and on how accustomed the one praying
has become to a time of silence. In general, try for a full minute
of silence. That will seem long at first and you may have to work
up to it. There is no need for a stopwatch. Just let the one who is
to lead the prayer after the silence be responsible so that the
others can simply relax and enjoy the quiet together. Trying for
the same length at every prayer can allow people to let go and
be free of wondering how long the silent time is going to last.

For good silence there must also be stillness. No moving
around. That means that people should be comfortable. Usually, they will be seated. Many people find it most helpful to sit
up straight, feet flat on the floor, hands resting loose on the lap,
all muscles relaxed. Should the eyes be opened or closed? Again
most persons find it easiest to reflect in silence when the eyes are
either closed or are gazing at one point, perhaps a candle or a
cross or whatever is in the center of the group.

Sometimes it helps to focus the mind also. One way to do this
is to recall one word or one phrase or sentence from the scripture or psalm just completed. Simply repeat these words over
and over, slowly, as your breath goes in and out. Don't necessar-
ily try to analyze the words, or figure out how they apply. Just
let them work in the silence. If no word or sentence has remained with you, then take a word like *Jesus,* or a phrase like
"Come, Holy Spirit" and repeat this over and over as you keep
the silence. Parents can learn to do this, then help their children
with it.

During the whole time of prayer, no more artificial light than
is necessary should be used. This is especially important for
times of silence.

Somehow we have come to think of silence as an absence of
sound, a negative thing, to be fought against with radios and
television and piped-in music and conversation no matter how
deadly. We learned to be uncomfortable with silence, and we
pass on this discomfort to children. But praying in common
knows silence as a presence, something positive, as filled with
beauty as any sound could be. That has to be experienced,
learned. It does not come all at once. After a whole Lent of

allowing a minute or more of silence in each day's prayer one begins to know what silence can be.

Words, Books and Scriptures

Words, for all their problems, do play a great part in praying. But we use them in a way that is quite different from when we are conversing about the weather or giving instructions or reporting on how the day went. Words in prayer are more like words used in poetry where they simply open up possibilities. They don't say it all, they only hint at things and leave much to the listener.

Consider a line of poetry like Emily Dickinson's "Hope is a thing with feathers." Now that's not the way we talk when we tell the salesperson what kind of shoes we want. And it isn't even true, in a literal sort of way: hope isn't a thing at all, and so feathers are out of the question. Yet there are facts and there are facts. And, for many, Dickinson's words say more about what they know hope to be in their hearts than any dictionary definition. That suggests something of how words are to be used in praying. They don't so much communicate information as a deeper truth that catches up our whole person: heart and soul and mind and body.

There are other images to help us understand words in prayer. Think of a high-school football game and how words are used by cheerleaders and the crowd. "Gimme a *W!*" And the crowd roars *W!* And on until the word is spelled and then repeated several times, louder and louder. Words here are part of the spirit. Again, they are not so important in themselves, in any information they communicate, as in what they do for this spirit: how they build it up, how they bring the crowd together, how they create an environment of support for the team. Words in prayer are sometimes like this. *Amen* and *Alleluia* and *Hosanna* are not information-giving words, they are acclamations, the words that draw us together. They aren't meant to be spoken the same way one says, "Pass the salt, please." They are rallying points.

When this book is used by several persons praying together, it is not necessary for all to have copies of the book. One may have a Bible to do the scripture reading, and another will have this book. When, at the start of a new season, a new prayer is begun, others will need to learn a few short phrases, a verse or two of a song. These can be memorized early in the season and then come quite easily. Words in prayer do their work when free of the book.

What of the psalms, then, that form an essential part of these prayers? Again, special efforts at learning the psalm have to be made during the first days of a season when the psalm is new. Ordinarily, a number of psalms are provided for each season so that those who are going to pray can select the one they consider most fitting. During the long months of ordinary time, a group might decide to use one psalm for a month, another the next month, and so on. Once a psalm is chosen, it will probably be necessary for everyone to have the words during the first days of the new season. A good way to do this is for the group to sit down around a table for a few minutes before the psalm is to be used for the first time. Each person needs a pen or pencil and a piece of paper, perhaps heavy paper that can stand some use. As the leader of the day's prayer reads the psalm slowly, each person writes it down. These copies can then be kept with the book and used at prayer. Very soon, most people will find they need the copy less and less: they have memorized a new prayer. The papers can then be put aside, while the leader keeps the text from the book as a memory aid.

Sometimes, when a psalm is to be used only a few times, it is presented here to be read by one person, with the others repeating one verse after each stanza. Such a way could be adapted to all the psalms, though generally they can be prayed well by all together, or by alternating verses with adults/children, men/women, or leader/others. When the reading of scripture is not to be part of the prayer, then one person might read the psalm slowly while the others listen.

Many of the words in our prayer come from the Bible. Of these, most used in the actual reading of scriptures within the prayers are of a "storytelling" variety. They are stories in a broad sense. Sometimes they do tell a story: creation, David and Goliath, the good Samaritan. Sometimes, though, it is not quite so clear: a geneology, the commandments, Jesus talking to his disciples the night before he died, Paul exhorting a church somewhere not to lose faith. These are stories in that they tell our own story, each a part of how we got to be who we are.

Scriptures have the kind of truth mentioned above in speaking of poetry: they tell stories that are more real to us, to who we are, have been, are becoming, than are the facts in the newspaper. Little by little we learn to listen to them as our own story. The one who does the scripture reading within the prayers should do so as a storyteller, repeating to this little church something of its own identity. For this to be effective, the reader must use a text which can be easily read. A good translation of the Bible is thus a necessary companion to this book. Scripture readings for every day of the year are given in the appropriate places. In a family setting, it will usually be possible for everyone who can read to take a turn with the Bible, but it is important that the reader look over the selection before the prayer so that it can be read well. Rotating the privilege of reading the scripture aloud also begins to give children some familiarity with the books of the Bible. At the conclusion of any scripture reading the reader may say, "This is the word of the Lord," and everyone answers "Thanks be to God."

The part of scripture that has always been used most extensively in Jewish and Christian public prayer is the book of Psalms. There are 150 psalms composed over a period of many centuries, long before the time of Jesus. Jesus himself, as a religious Jew, certainly used them constantly in his own prayers.

The psalms cover every sort of situation and emotion. Some psalms speak of affliction and persecution, some of victory, others of peace and work and family. There are angry psalms, joyful psalms, despairing psalms, exuberant psalms, calm psalms. There are psalms to teach, to praise, to thank, to celebrate. Some are for quiet moments of meditation, some for drum-beating, cymbal-clanging moments of leaping and dancing. Some are for the last moment before sleep, some for the first moment of a new day. Some were intended for use at special events: a wedding, the enthronement of a new king, an annual festival of harvest. Some were simply the everyday gratitude of the everyday person.

Many psalms will seem fine prayers the very first time we meet them. Others take some getting used to. Yet all have a strength. In part this strength must be the way praying the psalms joins our voices with our ancestors in faith, saints and unknowns, through thousands of years, before Jesus and after. Even more, the strength must be in the way these prayers can pass beyond the superficial things that change from one century to the next and touch on what remains the same about being human and putting trust in the Lord: things like our need for friends, our joy in the gifts of the earth, our loves and hates, our grief at loss, our sense of the quickness of life, our fear of what we do not understand, our failing and our sorrow.

The book of Psalms has been the constant prayer book of Christian and Jew. Verses of the psalms permeate our public prayers and the psalms constitute the greater part of all forms of morning and evening prayer. Yet the psalms were little used in the formation of those Christians who are adults today. Often the prayers which we learned as children were more recent compositions which have not endured so well. But if we now turn to the psalms, they are as new to us as to our children. Here and there we find familiar lines: "The Lord is my shepherd," or "From the depth I cry to you." But for the most part, the psalms are a new experience. And the words may seem strange at first: strong, straight talk at times, not so sweet as the prayers we grew up with. But the language of the psalms is honest and human and fresh after more than a hundred generations. If we have often left praying to the professionals and found it not at ease on our lips, the psalms could change that. They could be the source of a whole vocabulary of prayer for us and for our children so that prayer can no longer be reserved for the services on Sunday, the baptism or the funeral, but overflow to every day with the psalms we have memorized and made our own.

Only a few of the psalms are found in this book, and in some cases only parts of long psalms have been included. The selection has been based largely on the tradition of using the psalms that have most often been associated with a particular season.

Gestures

Prayer in common is not a gathering of bodiless spirits. It is persons with hearts and souls and minds and bodies. It all comes together. And the best prayers have been those that let the whole person get involved. Think of the rain dance of native Americans, of the Passover meal, of pilgrims in Jerusalem walking and kneeling as they make the way of the cross. Such prayer comes when there is no holding back, then the rite is such that it calls forth every bit of us. Some churches have preserved some of the richness that the body brings to prayer: genuflecting, bowing, folding the hands, kneeling, making the sign of the cross in various ways, processions, striking the breast, extending the hand in a sign of peace.

Yet, except for kneeling down and perhaps making the sign of the cross, we have seldom allowed ourselves to get involved bodily in our prayer at home. It is now rare for a parent to bless a child with hand on head or with the cross on the forehead or the heart. Prayer, when it cannot have our whole self, when it gets reduced to just the mind, loses its own strength, withers up, and we quite naturally cease to give it a place in our lives.

The prayers here will often suggest a posture (sitting, kneeling, standing) and will occasionally suggest some gesture. For example: extending the hands, palms down, in blessing; lifting the arms in praise; bowing deeply in adoration. A series of gestures may be suggested to go with a song. Of course, all suggestions for such gestures can be ignored. But in most cases if they are given a chance, used for a number of times until they come quite naturally, a person will begin to understand why they are there. Gesture adds a dimension to our prayer that cannot be obtained in any other way.

It is important that everyone who prays also participates in gesture, whether it be a blessing or simply the sign of the cross. Only when all are participants can common gesture do its task. This is a feeling for the unity of the group, be it two people or a dozen, be they all adults or four generations. To fold hands together, to raise the hands and join them, to bow or kneel all as one goes beyond any intellectual conviction that the many are one and puts that conviction into our bones.

On occasion, when a verse or a hymn is to be used throughout a season, someone in the family could plan and teach a set of gestures to accompany the speaking or the singing. In doing this, listen to the sound of the piece as well as to the words and keep the gestures and the flow of movement very simple.

In adding "new" gestures, be careful to keep the old, familiar gestures in all their beauty. The sign of the cross, for example, with or without words, could always mark the beginning of prayer.

Things

Songs and silences, words and gestures. There is at least one other element in our prayer together. That is partly a function of where we pray, the place for prayer discussed above. But something should be said about the objects which form a part of our prayer.

Like words, the things around us can work on different levels. The bread that fills our stomachs and keeps us going can also be the bearer of unity among humans. By being a focus for our eyes, or something to touch with our hands or kiss with our lips as we break it and pass it in our blessing prayer, bread reveals not only itself as gift of God and work of human hands, but reveals and helps create the unity of the table.

Thus some of the prayers in this book have suggestions for the use of some object in the prayer: bread and wine at the Sunday-welcoming meal; the wreath at Advent prayers; the crèche or tree at Christmas; the cross or ashes during Lent; water in Eastertime. Perhaps one in the group will have a good feel for how such objects might be used. Simplicity is essential. The thing should not be lost by having too much of it, or too much display. It is enough, for example, that there be a clear bowl filled with water and placed on a bright piece of fabric. When nothing special is called for in the prayer, then a plant or a flower or a candle or something else simple and beautiful can be placed at the center of the prayer space.

When water is to be taken to make the sign of the cross, or when wine is to be passed from hand to hand, when anything at all is to be touched (including this book or the book of scriptures), it should be touched with reverence. Not because what is used in prayer is somehow sacred and therefore different from any other water or wine, but because in prayer we are acknowledging a sacredness that resides in all creation—in all that is natural and all that has been shaped with care by others. This reverence should not be something phony, but should flow from the atmosphere of the prayer which says that there need be no rushing, no carelessness. Nor is reverence deadly and solemn. It is joyful, eager, smiling. When one hands a piece of the broken bread to another, it is not so much that something necessary is being done, but something that is *un*necessary, therefore special. And so one takes care to place the bread into the other's hand, to touch and hold the hand for a moment, to look at the other person.

These gestures which involve objects are often the heart of our common prayer. At the eucharist the central act of prayer is our eating and drinking of the bread and wine that has been blessed. At baptism, it is the immersion in water. These are the symbols of our life together as Christians. So in our prayer at home, the kissing of the cross or the sharing of the cup or the signing with water are vital to our prayer's ability to center this household and confirm its faith.

And All Together
The whole is more than the sum of its parts. The prayer we do together is not really just adding up words, silences, songs, things, gestures. It is the back and forth, the flow of all these together in patterns that we become comfortable with. Balance is crucial. Words can get out of control and dominate, especially at first when we may be uneasy about gestures, singing and such. You may also find that for your situation the prayers need to be changed a little or a lot. They are yours. Keep in mind what has been said of the need for prayer to reach all our many sides and to draw them into the praying.

The Leader of Prayer
When the group is small and the prayer is of a simple structure, then the task of a leader is not difficult. The leader is to know the movement of the prayer very well; he or she should give thought beforehand to anything that is particular to the prayer of that day and should see that all is ready. Prayer is difficult

when no one knows what comes next. It is much more possible when, even on the first time through in a new season, there is the feeling that one person has the flow in mind so well that such concerns do not hinder the prayer even for that person. It makes all the difference.

There are ways to divide up the leadership in prayer. In the Sunday-welcoming meal, for example, one lights the Sabbath candles and says the blessing, another raises the cup of wine and says that blessing. Or in the usual morning or evening prayer, the one who reads the scripture will be someone other than the one leading the whole prayer. In a family with young children, parents should be sure that even the youngest child takes a turn at some task: leading a short acclamation or holding the holy water for everyone. Children should not be forced; often they only want to be sure they really have the trust of the parents. Adults must give full attention when a child reads the scripture.

The leadership in prayer in a small group would normally rotate from one person to another. Sunday, marking the beginning of a new week, would usually be the day to change the leader.

More than anything else, the leader is a leader of prayer. That is the only reason he or she needs to know what comes when and who does what: so that all are free to pray. Prayer has many spirits—serious and light, sad and joyful, fearful and confident. The leader senses the mood of the moment. A leader is not to keep it all serious, all heavy and straight-faced. Good order and a sense of the group allow for prayer to have its moments of spontaneity.

In the household, each person is important for the prayer. No one is a spectator for such is deadly to the possibility of prayer. When the prayer comes in such a way that each person, adult and child, senses his/her importance, then coming together to pray will, each day, be a re-creation of the spirit in that home.

Chapter 1

✛✛✛

THE DAILY PRAYER

Introduction

There are four times of the day when prayer seems possible: morning, evening, mealtime and bedtime. Perhaps at one or two of these times a family could regularly gather for some prayer together. For the others, some single prayer might be memorized for private prayer.

Throughout Jewish tradition and Christian tradition, morning and evening have always been the daily times to pray—to praise God at dawn, to thank God at nightfall. In the psalms and other prayers we continue to stand in that tradition, praying what prophets, apostles, ordinary folks and Jesus himself prayed.

Saint Basil the Great said of morning prayer: ". . . we may take nothing in hand until we have been gladdened by the thought of God . . . or set our bodies to any task before we do what has been said: 'I will pray to you, Lord, you will hear my voice in the morning; I will stand before you in the morning and gaze on you.'" Basil was quoting Psalm 5. There are morning prayers here for private use by adults and by children; these are the "Morning Prayers for the Individual" and "Morning Prayers for the Young Person." They are for quiet prayer while rising and dressing and for use any day of the year. Just one of these short prayers might be chosen at the beginning, and others added gradually. These prayers do what Basil suggests, they gladden us with the thought of God from the moment our eyes are open.

The "Morning Prayer Together" and the "Evening Prayer Together," while they could be used by an individual, are arranged for two or more to pray together. These are for the weekdays of Ordinary Time. Ordinary Time refers to those weeks of the year that are not a part of Advent, Christmastime, Lent or Eastertime. In some Christian traditions this is the Pentecost or Trinity season. Thus Ordinary Time begins on the day after the second Sunday in January and lasts until the Tuesday before Ash Wednesday; it begins again on the day after Pentecost and goes all the way to the day before Advent starts. Daily prayer for the special seasons will be found within each season in following sections of this book.

Because Ordinary Time lasts so long, options have been provided in the hymns and psalms so that a change can be made every month or so. When scripture is to be read as part of the morning or evening prayer, the selections assigned to each day by the lectionary are found in Appendix II. The reader will need to know only what week of Ordinary Time it is; the Sunday liturgy will be the best guide and reminder. As everywhere in this book, feel free to shorten or lengthen these morning and evening prayers to meet needs.

The third occasion of daily prayer is at meals. Here we remember and affirm that thanksgiving is what faith invites from all of life. The meal is the obvious occasion to express this. The meal prayers included simply suggest some of the words, music and gestures that can be used to bless God for the food and for the gathering at the table. Some of the seasonal sections have additional suggestions for meal prayers. All such prayers strive to give some sign for the spirit that gathers us and fills us at table, and to strengthen that spirit.

Finally, there is the prayer for the night, for bedtime. This again is a quiet and private sort of devotion, one which could well remain the same every night of the year, though alternatives to the psalm and the prayer have been provided.

Daily prayer blends what is quickly familiar and committed to memory with what is special to each day. The scripture alone is new each time as we the church tell our story through several years. The rest, except for a new psalm or song when we feel the need, becomes as comfortable and rich as the Lord's Prayer or the Creed. Even the psalms are quickly memorized. The special seasons as they come, Advent through Eastertime, provide a rhythm to the year and its prayer, touching old and new parts of ourselves and our faith. The ordinary prayer of the ordinary time, however, remains the strong, simple prayer that sustains us.

Morning Prayer

The prayer of morning is always the prayer of praise. It is called forth by the rising sun: our world is light again. We are rising like the sun. Nothing can be imagined that would so strongly bring home what has happened: Christ is risen; sin and death, which the nighttime seemed to shelter, are defeated. Life, even during the daylight, may be filled with the works of darkness, with hardship, hurt, sadness, ingratitude, frustration. But morning prayer proclaims that praise which knows that God's love will prevail.

Morning, like most parts of most days, has been filled with deadlines. We must accomplish a good many things in the hour after rising, and by then the household is dispersed. Prayer, which needs room to breathe, hardly seems at home here. Yet, for Christians, there is hardly a more important time to pray. Starting the day, alone or together, without praying is to test one's faith. To praise God, at the start, to frame the day in thanksgiving, to proclaim the kind of world it is whatever the events of later on might try to say—that is why we pray at the start of things.

> For Christians the beginning of the day should not be burdened and oppressed with besetting concerns for the day's work. At the threshold of the new day stands the Lord who made it. All the darkness and distraction of the dreams of night retreat before the clear light of Jesus Christ and his wakening Word. All unrest, all impurity, all care and anxiety flee before him. Therefore, at the beginning of the day let all distraction and empty talk be silenced and let the first thought and the first word belong to him to whom our

whole life belongs. "Awake thou that sleepest, and arise from the dead, and Christ shall give thee light" (Eph. 5:14).

(*Dietrich Bonhoeffer in* Life Together)

Some of the private prayers which follow are much like the morning prayers that would have been familiar to Jesus, his parents and his disciples. They are taken in part from the Jewish daily prayerbook. The form for prayer together includes the invitation to pray, a song, a psalm, a reading from scripture (or this could be part of the evening prayer), some silence, a prayer. Morning prayer together might take place at the bedside, or at the breakfast table, or at a window facing east. It will probably be possible only when the family agrees that it will be at some set moment (on rising, before breakfast, at a specific time) and when it is begun on time and kept very brief.

Morning Prayers for the Individual

The following may be silent prayers at the first moments of the day.

On opening the eyes:
> Blessed are you, Lord, God of all creation,
> for you open the eyes of the blind.

On rising:
> Blessed are you, Lord, God of all creation,
> for you raise up those who are bowed down.
> Blessed are you, Lord, God of all creation,
> for you set captives free.

On standing up:
> Blessed are you, Lord, God of all creation,
> for you fashioned us in wisdom and endowed us with health
> and you do wonders.

On dressing:
> Blessed are you, Lord, God of all creation,
> for you clothe the naked.

On the first steps of the day:
> Blessed are you, Lord, God of all creation,
> for you guide our steps.

On washing:
> Blessed are you, Lord, God of all creation,
> for you remove sleep from my eyes and slumber from my
> eyelids.

On going to breakfast:
> Blessed are you, Lord, God of all creation,
> for you provide for all my needs.

On going outside:
> Blessed are you, Lord, God of all creation,
> for you stretch out the earth upon the waters.

One of the following morning prayers could also be learned.
> We give you thanks, almighty God,
> because in you we have rested in sleep,
> and to you we have risen after rest.
> Awaken your grace in us always
> and let the splendor of your brightness
> shine all through us.
> Then, by striving, we may come to the path
> which leads to your light.

> In mercy you give light to the earth
> and to those who dwell on it.
> In your goodness you renew the work of creation every
> day, constantly.

> Hear, O Israel, the Lord is our God, the Lord is one.
> Blessed be the name of his glorious majesty forever and
> ever.
> You shall love the Lord your God with all your heart,
> and with all your soul and with all your might.
> And these words which I command you today shall be in
> your heart.
> You shall teach them diligently to your children,
> and you shall speak of them when you are sitting at home
> and when you go on a journey,
> when you lie down and when you rise up.

Morning Prayers for a Young Person

Any of the thanksgiving prayers ("Blessed are you . . .") from
the preceding section would be appropriate for the child, or any
of the following could be learned by heart a little at a time.

Glory be to the Father and to the Son and to the Holy
Spirit—as it was in the beginning, is now and ever shall be,
world without end. Amen.

I arise today through the strength of heaven:
light of the sun,
radiance of the moon,
splendor of fire,
speed of lightning,
swiftness of the wind,
depth of the sea,
stability of the earth,
firmness of the rock.

I arise today through God's strength to pilot me,
God's might to uphold me,
God's wisdom to guide me,
God's eye to look before me,
God's ear to hear me,
God's word to speak for me,
God's hand to guard me,
God's way to lie before me.

(Lorica of Saint Patrick)

To you I pray, O Lord;
   at dawn you hear my voice;
   at dawn I bring my plea expectantly
      before you.

(Psalm 5:3–4)

Morning Prayer Together

When everyone is together, the leader begins. All make the sign of the cross in silence, then in response to the leader's first words of invitation to prayer, all may raise their hands to shoulder level, palms up, arms somewhat extended in front of the body. This posture could be held through the morning song. Note that only one song is sung; the leader selects from the several choices here. Alternate psalms are given following the morning prayer.

Call to prayer

Leader: Come, let us praise the Lord.
   All: And sing of our salvation.

Song

(*1*) Holy, Holy, Holy, Lord God almighty!
     Early in the morning our song shall rise to thee;
     Holy, Holy, Holy, merciful and mighty;
     God in three persons, blessed Trinity!

(*Reginald Heber*)

(*2*) *To the tune of "Morning Has Broken":*

This day God sends me	God's way is my way,
Strength of high heaven,	God's shield is round me,
Sun and moon shining,	God's hosts defend me,
Flame in my hearth,	Saving from ill.
Flashing of lightning,	Angels of heaven,
Wind in its swiftness,	Drive from me always
Deeps of the ocean,	All that would harm me;
Firmness of earth.	Stand by me still.

(*J. Quinn*)

(*3*) *To the tune of "Praise God From Whom All Blessings Flow":*
     Now that the daylight fills the sky,
     We lift our hearts to God on high,
     That he, in all we do or say,
     May keep us free from harm this day.

(4) Especially in summertime, the hymn "Morning Has Broken" is appropriate.

Psalm 148:1–3, 7–13
This psalm, or one of those given on the following pages, is prayed by all together or by two groups alternating.

Praise the Lord from the heavens,
    praise him in the heights;
Praise him, all you his angels,
    praise him, all you his hosts.
Praise him, sun and moon;
    praise him, all you shining stars.

Praise the Lord from the earth,
    you sea monsters and all depths;
Fire and hail, snow and mist,
    storm winds that fulfill his word;
You mountains and all you hills,
    you fruit trees and all you cedars;
You wild beasts and all tame animals,
    you creeping things and you winged fowl.

Let the kings of the earth and all peoples,
    the princes and all the judges of the earth,
Young men too, and maidens,
    old men and boys,
Praise the name of the Lord,
    for his name alone is exalted.

Scripture
The daily scripture may be read now or at some other time during the day. All are seated. The scripture readings for the weekdays of Ordinary Time are found in Appendix II.

Silence
After the scripture (or the psalm if the scripture is not read) all remain seated in silence for some time.

Prayer

All stand. The following prayer, or one composed by the leader, may be used.

Leader: We call to you, Lord of mercy.

   All: God of all comfort.

Leader: Let us pray.

> Our Father, grant peace, blessing and grace.
> Bless us, O our Father, all of us together,
> with the light of your presence.
> By that light you have given us loving-kindness,
> righteousness, life and peace . . .
>> *(Other gifts of God may be mentioned here.)*
> O may it be good in your sight at all times
> to bless all your children with your peace.
> We ask this in the name of Jesus the Lord.

   All: Amen.

Doxology

All may bow deeply for the first part of this prayer.

All: Glory be to the Father and to the Son and to the Holy
    Spirit—as it was in the beginning, is now, and ever shall be,
    world without end. Amen.

Alternate Psalms

The following psalms are also appropriate for morning prayer.
If one is chosen it should be used over several weeks.

Psalm 67

> May God have pity on us and bless us;
>> may he let his face shine upon us.
> So may your way be known upon earth;
>> among all nations, your salvation.
> May the peoples praise you, O God;
>> may all the peoples praise you.
> May the nations be glad and exult
>> because you rule the peoples in equity;
>> the nations on the earth you guide.

May the peoples praise you, O God;
>   may all the peoples praise you!
The earth has yielded its fruits;
>   God, our God, has blessed us.
May God bless us,
>   and may all the ends of the earth fear him!

Psalm 146:1–2, 5–10

Praise the Lord, O my soul;
>   I will praise the Lord all my life;
>   I will sing praise to my God while I live.
Happy he whose help is the God of Jacob,
>   whose hope is in the Lord, his God,
Who made heaven and earth,
>   the sea and all that is in them;
Who keeps faith forever,
>   secures justice for the oppressed,
>   gives food to the hungry.
The Lord sets captives free;
>   the Lord gives sight to the blind.
The Lord raises up those that were bowed down;
>   the Lord loves the just.
The Lord protects strangers;
>   the fatherless and the widow he sustains,
>   but the way of the wicked he thwarts.
The Lord shall reign forever;
>   your God, O Zion, through all generations. Alleluia!

Daniel 3:57–59, 62–66, 69, 71–76, 78–81, 85

This is prayed as a litany. One person speaks each verse and all respond: "Praise and exalt him above all forever."

Bless the Lord, all you works of the Lord,
praise and exalt him above all forever.
Angels of the Lord, bless the Lord:
You heavens, bless the Lord:
Sun and moon, bless the Lord:
Stars of heaven, bless the Lord:
Every shower and dew, bless the Lord:

All you winds, bless the Lord:
Fire and heat, bless the Lord:
Frost and chill, bless the Lord:
Nights and days, bless the Lord:
Light and darkness, bless the Lord:
Lightnings and clouds, bless the Lord:
Let the earth bless the Lord:
Mountains and hills, bless the Lord:
Everything growing from the earth, bless the Lord:
Seas and rivers, bless the Lord:
You dolphins and all water creatures, bless the Lord:
All you birds of the air, bless the Lord:
All you beasts, wild and tame, bless the Lord:
Servants of the Lord, bless the Lord:

Evening Prayer

The prayer of evening is the prayer of thanks. It is, like morning prayer, a great "hinge" of our day; it is the moment when concerns about responsibilities can change to joy in a meal together, in conversation, in pursuit of what interests and challenges us, in relaxation, in play, in rest. Such an evening is not without its threats, however: we know that emptiness on one side and frenzy on the other destroy the evening time for many.

The church's prayer at evening, from earliest years as it came from the evening prayer of Israel, is giving thanks for the day just past and asking protection in the darkness. It begins in praise of light, the great light that has filled our world all day and the little light which we kindle for ourselves in the evening. In these lights we praise Jesus Christ who is light of the world.

The structure of this prayer is similar to that of the morning, but it begins with the lighting of the candle or lamp and the praise of Jesus. The song, psalm, scripture and silence follow. Then comes a traditional element of evening prayer, the intercession. Several options are given for this. Evening prayer ends with a blessing. Several possible songs are given within the service and a number of alternatives for the psalm follow the service.

A time should be selected that can be kept consistently. A fine candle is placed in the center of the group; there should be little else around it. The lighting of this candle is a part of the prayer, not something to be done beforehand. It should be done with reverence. Other lights should be kept low.

Call to Prayer

When all are standing ready, one lights the candle in silence, then says or sings:

Jesus Christ is the light of the world. Alleluia!

And everyone responds:

A light no darkness can put out. Alleluia!

Song

(*1*) Now thank we all our God
With heart and hands and voices,
Who wondrous things has done,
In whom his world rejoices,
Who from our mothers' arms
Has blessed us on our way
With countless gifts of love
And still is ours today.

(Martin Rinckart)

(*2*) *To the tune of "Praise God From Whom All Blessings Flow" or any tune to that meter:*

O radiant Light, O Sun divine
Of God the Father's deathless face,
O Image of the light sublime
That fills the heav'nly dwelling place.

Lord Jesus Christ, as daylight fades,
As shine the lights of eventide,
We praise the Father with the Son,
The Spirit blest and with them one.

("Phos Hilarion," the ancient Greek evening hymn,
translated by Wm. Storey)

(3) To the tune of "Joyful, Joyful," or "Praise the Lord, Ye Heavens Adore Him" or any tune of that meter:

Thy strong word did cleave the darkness;
At thy speaking it was done;
For created light we thank thee,
While thine ordered seasons run:
Alleluia! Alleluia!
Praise to thee, who light dost send!
Alleluia! Alleluia!
Alleluia without end!

Give us lips to sing thy glory,
Tongues thy mercy to proclaim,
Throats that shout the hope that fills us,
Mouths to speak thy holy name:
Alleluia! Alleluia!
May the light which thou dost send
Fill our songs with Alleluias
Alleluias without end.

(Martin Franzman)

(4) He's got the whole world in his hands;
He's got the whole wide world in his hands;
He's got the whole world in his hands;
He's got the whole world in his hands.

He's got the setting sun . . .

He's got the light and darkness . . .

(5) Kumbaya, my Lord, kumbaya,
Kumbaya, my Lord, kumbaya,
Kumbaya, my Lord, kumbaya,
O Lord, kumbaya.

Psalm 121

This psalm, or one given on the following pages, is prayed by all together or by two groups alternating.

> I lift up my eyes toward the mountains;
>> whence shall help come to me?
> My help is from the Lord,
>> who made heaven and earth.
> May he not suffer your foot to slip;
>> may he slumber not who guards you:
> Indeed he neither slumbers nor sleeps,
>> the guardian of Israel.
> The Lord is your guardian; the Lord is your shade;
>> he is beside you at your right hand.
> The sun shall not harm you by day,
>> nor the moon by night.
> The Lord will guard you from all evil;
>> he will guard your life.
> The Lord will guard your coming and your going,
>> both now and forever.

Scripture

The daily scripture may be read now. All are seated. Scripture readings for the weekdays of Ordinary Time will be found in Appendix II.

Silence

After the scripture (or after the psalm if the scripture is not read now) all sit in silence for a time.

Prayers of Intercession

If time allows, prayers of intercession are offered now. One form is given here. Some may wish simply to speak various intentions and concerns. A short moment of silence should follow each prayer.

> Remember, O Lord, this city wherein we dwell and every other city and country and all who dwell in them.
> Remember, O Lord, all who travel.
> Remember, O Lord, all who labor under sickness or slavery; remember them for health and safety.

Remember, O Lord, those in your holy church who bring
forth good fruit, are rich in good works and forget
not the poor.
(Other prayers may be added.)
Grant unto us all your mercy and loving kindness,
and grant that we may with one mouth and one heart
praise and glorify your great and glorious name,
Father, Son and Holy Spirit, now, henceforth and for ever.
(From a prayer of John Chrysostom)

The Lord's Prayer
All stand and join hands and pray the Our Father. Continue with hands joined for the blessing.

Blessing
Leader: May the Lord bless us and keep us.
  All: Amen.
Leader: May his face shine upon us and be gracious to us.
  All: Amen.
Leader: May he look on us with kindness and give us his peace.
  All: Amen.

Alternate Psalms

Psalm 8:2, 4–10
O Lord, our Lord,
  how glorious is your name over all the earth!
You have exalted your majesty above the heavens.
When I behold your heavens, the work of your fingers,
  the moon and the stars which you set in place—
What is man that you should be mindful of him,
  or the son of man that you should care for him?
You have made him little less than the angels,
  and crowned him with glory and honor.
You have given him rule over the works of your hands,
  putting all things under his feet:
All sheep and oxen,
  yes, and the beasts of the field,

The birds of the air, the fishes of the sea,
 and whatever swims the paths of the seas.
O Lord, our Lord,
 how glorious is your name over all the earth!

The Song of Mary: Luke 1:46–55

"My being proclaims the greatness of the Lord,
 my spirit finds joy in God my savior.
For he has looked upon his servant in her lowliness;
 all ages to come shall call me blessed.
God who is mighty has done great things for me,
 holy is his name;
His mercy is from age to age
 on those who fear him.
He has shown might with his arm;
 he has confused the proud in their inmost thoughts.
He has deposed the mighty from their thrones
 and raised the lowly to high places.
The hungry he has given every good thing,
 while the rich he has sent empty away.
He has upheld Israel his servant,
 ever mindful of his mercy;
Even as he promised our fathers,
 promised Abraham and his descendants forever."

Alternate Intercessions

In peace, let us pray to the Lord.

For an evening that is perfect, holy, peaceful and without sin, let us pray to the Lord.

For an angel of peace, a faithful guide and guardian of our souls and bodies, let us pray to the Lord.

For all that is good and profitable to our souls and for the peace of the world, let us pray to the Lord.

For peace and repentance for sin throughout the rest of our lives, let us pray to the Lord.

For a peaceful and Christian end to our lives, without shame or pain, and for a good defense before the awesome judgment seat of Christ, let us pray to the Lord.

Help, save, pity and defend us, O God, by your grace.
(*Other prayers may be spoken here*.)

Meal Prayers

We hunger in body and spirit and we are fed with food and with fellowship at table. In the basic beauty and simplicity of this comes the understanding of eucharist, the gathering of Christians to bless, break and share bread, to bless and share the cup. The holiness of eucharist is known only through the holiness of our meals. At table we always thank God for the gifts of food and of each other. The blessing at our table can take many forms, but all of them are to be this thanks and praise.

The blessing is honest when it is given honor, when we graciously wait upon one another, when we are conscious that our table is but one part of the dining table of all the earth at which many are hungry, when we share our words and our attention with all at the table, when our appreciation overflows into the work of preparation and cleaning.

Following are some forms for prayer at table. Others will be found in the sections on Sunday (for the Sunday-welcoming meal of Saturday night), Advent, Christmastime, Lent and Eastertime. Sometimes the form for Evening Prayer may serve as a meal prayer. If this is done, those parts before the scripture reading might precede the meal, with the scripture, silence and prayers of intercession following the meal.

Whatever form is used, it is often best to have one short verse or word to begin. This could be a phrase taken from any of these blessings, with the parent or leader speaking the first few words and all responding. Or it could be as simple as the verse that leads into the blessing at the eucharist:

Leader: Let us give thanks to the Lord our God.
All: It is right to give him thanks and praise.

1. *This traditional form of blessing could be prayed with hands joined or with hands extended in blessing over the food.*
   Bless us, O Lord, and these thy gifts
   which we are about to receive through thy bounty;
   through Christ our Lord. Amen.

2. *Standing at table, all sing "Praise God" with the gestures described:*
  Praise God from whom all blessings flow;
(For this line, all extend their hands over the table in blessing.)
  Praise him all creatures here below;
(Here all join hands.)
  Praise him above ye heav'nly host;
(Raise hands, still joined, high in the air.)
  Praise Father, Son and Holy Ghost.
(Lower hands, still joined, and bow deeply.)

(Movements by Carla De Sola)

3.   Blessed are you, Lord, God of all creation,
      for you feed the whole world with your goodness,
      with grace, with loving kindness and tender mercy.
      You give food to all creatures,
      for your loving kindness endures forever.
      Because of your great goodness food has never failed us;
      O may it not fail us for ever and ever
      for the sake of your great name.
      You nourish and sustain all creatures and do good to all,
      Blessed are you, O Lord, for you give food to all.

4.   May the grace of our Lord Jesus Christ
      and the love of God
      and the fellowship of the Holy Spirit be with us all. Amen.

5.   We entreat you, O Lord, mercifully to bless the air and the
      dews,
      the rains and the winds;
      that through heavenly benediction
      all may be saved from dearth and famine,
      and enjoy the fruits of the earth in abundance and plenty;
      for the eyes of all wait upon you, O Lord,
      and you give them their food in due season.

(From an Indian prayer)

6. We plow the fields and scatter the good seed on the land,
    But it is fed and watered by God's almighty hand.
    He sends the snow in winter, the warmth to swell the grain,
    The breezes and the sunshine, and soft, refreshing rain.
        All good gifts around us are sent from heaven above;
        Then thank the Lord, O thank the Lord for all his love.

    We thank thee, then, O Father, for all things bright and
            good:
    The seed-time and the harvest, our life, our health, our
            food.
    Accept the gifts we offer, for all thy love imparts,
    And, what thou most desirest, our humble, thankful
            hearts.
        All good gifts around us are sent from heaven above;
        Then thank the Lord, O thank the Lord for all his love.
                                        (*Matthias Claudius*)

7. *Leader:* The eyes of all hope in you, Lord.
    All: And you give them food in due season.
   Leader: You open your hand,
    All: And every creature is filled with your blessings.
   Leader: Blessed is God in his gifts and holy in all his works.

8. *Leader:* The poor shall eat and be filled,
    All: And shall praise the Lord.
   Leader: The Lord is kind and compassionate.
    All: And gives food to those who fear him.
   Leader: Blessed is God in his gifts and holy in all his works.

9. Kumbaya, my Lord, kumbaya . . .
    Someone's praising, Lord, kumbaya . . .
    Someone's thanking, Lord, kumbaya . . .

10. Silence together can also be blessing, sometimes with hands
joined. A special way to conclude such a silence is for one person
to begin humming a steady note. Others begin also, but each at
a different pitch, whatever feels right. Let this continue for a
few moments. The harmony will be beautiful and will express
the union at table.

11. *Another song blessing:*
    We're gonna sit at the welcome table,
    We're gonna sit at the welcome table one of these
      days, Hallelujah,
    We're gonna sit at the welcome table,
    Gonna sit at the welcome table one of these days.

12. O Lord God, heavenly Father,
    bless unto us these thy gifts,
    which of thy tender kindness thou hast bestowed upon us,
    through Jesus Christ our Lord. Amen.

                                  (Martin Luther)

13. *A sung blessing to the tune of "Edelweiss":*
    Thanks to God, praise and thanks!
    Lord, we gather together.
    From the earth you have brought
    Bread to break now together.
    All who have hungered shall bless your name,
    Bless your name forever.
    Thanks to God, praise and thanks!
    Lord, you bring us together.

14. *This is a song of praise based on Psalm 148. It is sung to the tune of* *"Row, Row, Row Your Boat."*
    Praise God in the heights! Praise him on the earth!
    Praise, praise, praise, praise! Praise for all you're worth.

    Praise him sun and moon! Praise him shining stars!
    Hills, trees, creeping things, trains and planes and cars!

    Praise him, all the earth! Monsters of the deep!
    Fire, hail, frost, snow! Waking or asleep!

    Praise God in the loaf! Praise him in the root!
    Wheat, corn, barley, rye, vegetables and fruit.

15. *To the tune of "Praise God From Whom All Blessings Flow" or any
tune of the same meter:*
    Be present at our table, Lord.
    Be here and everywhere adored.
    Thy creatures bless and grant that we
    May feast in Paradise with thee.

    We thank thee, Lord, for this our food,
    For life and health and ev'ry good;
    By thine own hand may we be fed;
    Give us each day our daily bread.

    (John Cennick)

16. Especially at festive meals, fill all the glasses and propose a
toast as part of the blessing. For example: on a birthday, to the
one celebrating; on New Year's, to the good spirits of the year
ahead. Spontaneous toasts can be added.

17. *Holding up the bread, one prays:*
    Blessed are you, Lord, God of all creation,
    for you bring forth bread from the earth.
*Then the bread is passed and each person takes a piece. Then all eat
together. Sometimes it is customary to kiss the bread in silence.*

18. O Lord, bless this food created by you,
    that it may be a means of good health for us.
    Grant by this invocation of your holy name
    that all who partake of this food
    may receive health of body and protection of soul.

19. Each member of the household can be responsible for the
meal blessing for a week at a time. The blessing can be a traditional one, a reading, a made-up prayer, or other appropriate
forms of prayer.

20. Blessed are you, O God,
    for you have nourished me from my youth,
    and you give food to all creatures.

After the meal:

1.   Blessed is God of whose bounty we have partaken.
    Blessed be God through whose goodness we live.

2.   Blessed are you, O Lord our God,
    for you have nourished us since our infancy,
    and with us all that breathe.
    Fill our hearts with joy,
    that we may abound in all kinds of good works,
    through Jesus Christ our Lord,
    to whom with thee and the Holy Spirit
    be glory, honor and power. Amen.

Night Prayer

This is a bedside prayer, a final prayer before sleep. Parts of it may be used when praying with young children at night. Additional psalms and prayers are given following the basic form; these psalms are a most ancient part of the church's night prayer.

This is the quiet prayer of an individual, but it could also be prayed by two or more together, alternating the verses of the psalm or saying it together.

The night with its darkness and weariness touches us with fear, with anxiety even, but also with confidence. More than any other prayer, the night prayer is that of the child speaking to the parent, secure even in the fearsome dark. We need no reminders to associate the night with death, this short sleep with our final sleep in the Lord. It is not simply the thought "If I should die before I wake . . ."; rather, the night and sleep are a way of learning to die, to commend ourselves to the Lord over and over again until we are ready to do it a last time.

The prayer begins after some silent moments of reflection on the day that has ended: in praise of God's gifts, in sorrow for any wrong we have done. The prayer could be said kneeling, or even after getting into bed.

(Making the sign of the cross:)

    May the Lord give us a quiet night and a good death.

O Lord, my heart is not proud,
   nor are my eyes haughty;
I busy not myself with great things,
   nor with things too sublime for me.
Nay rather, I have stilled and quieted
   my soul like a weaned child.
Like a weaned child on its mother's lap,
   [so is my soul within me.]
   O Israel, hope in the Lord,
   both now and forever.

(Psalm 131)

Keep us, O Lord, as the apple of your eye;
shelter us in the shadow of your wings.

Visit this home, we ask you, Lord.
Chase far from it all that leads to evil.
Send your holy angels here to keep us in peace.
May your blessing be always with us.

Alternate Psalms

Psalm 4

When I call, answer me, O my just God,
   you who relieve me when I am in distress;
   Have pity on me, and hear my prayer!
Men of rank, how long will you be dull of heart?
   Why do you love what is vain and seek after falsehood?
Know that the Lord does wonders for his faithful one;
   the Lord will hear me when I call upon him.
Tremble, and sin not;
   reflect, upon your beds, in silence.
Offer just sacrifices,
   and trust in the Lord.
Many say, "Oh, that we might see better times!"
   O Lord, let the light of your countenance shine upon
      us!
You put gladness into my heart,

more than when grain and wine abound.
As soon as I lie down, I fall peacefully asleep,
   for you alone, O Lord,
   bring security to my dwelling.

Psalm 134

Come, bless the Lord,
   all you servants of the Lord
Who stand in the house of the Lord
   during the hours of night.
Lift up your hands toward the sanctuary
   and bless the Lord.
May the Lord bless you from Zion,
   the maker of heaven and earth.

The Song of Simeon: Luke 2:29–32

"Now, Master, you can dismiss your servant in peace;
   you have fulfilled your word.
For my eyes have witnessed your saving deed
   displayed for all the peoples to see:
A revealing light to the Gentiles,
   the glory of your people Israel."

Other Prayers

Blessed are you, Lord, God of all creation,
for you make the brands of sleep to fall upon my eyes
and slumber on my eyelids.
May it be your will, O Lord my God and God of my
   ancestors,
to allow me to lie down in peace
and to let me rise up again in peace.
Let not my thoughts trouble me, nor fearful dreams,
but let my rest be perfect before you.

                             (*Jewish night prayer*)

Blessed be the Lord by day!
Blessed be the Lord by night!
Blessed be the Lord when we lie down!

Blessed be the Lord when we rise up!
For in your hands are all the souls of all the living and
    dead.
Into your hands, I commend my spirit.
You have redeemed me, O Lord God of truth.

*   (Jewish night prayer)*

O Lord our God, make us lie down in peace,
and raise us up, O our king, to life.

Chapter 2

✠✠✠

SUNDAY

Introduction: Keeping Sunday Holy

"Take care to keep holy the sabbath day as the Lord, your
God, commanded you.

Six days you may labor and do all your work; but the
seventh day is the sabbath of the Lord, your God.

No work may be done then, whether by you, or your son or
daughter, or your male or female slave, or your ox
or ass or any of your beasts, or the alien who lives
with you.

Your male and female slaves should rest as you do.

For remember that you too were once slaves in Egypt, and
the Lord, your God, brought you from there with
his strong hand and outstretched arm.

That is why the Lord, your God, has commanded you to
observe the sabbath day."

(Deuteronomy 5:12–15)

In our biblical tradition, the Sabbath as a different day
among the seven symbolizes who we believe we are: a free
people, liberated by the Lord. As the commandment shows,
making the day different was and is a way to take that freedom
from the history books and theology books and make it a matter
of present delight. For not only did this happen a long time ago
for our ancestors, but it is happening in our lives right now.

It was a radical thought those thousands of years ago to
issue a declaration of independence for one day in seven, it is

nearly unthinkable today. The work week may be down to five or even four days, but all seven days and nights aren't enough for most of us to finish our agendas. Slaveries of one sort may have passed away, but new kinds are always available. From one age to another, keeping Sabbath is a promise to remember the God who breaks the bonds of every slavery.

Jesus: The Sabbath Was Made for Us!

When we think of Jesus and the Sabbath, we remember the stories about people accusing him of breaking the Sabbath with his cures, or letting his disciples harvest some grain. Jesus had such a fine answer: "The Sabbath was made for people, not people for Sabbath."

Most often we miss the first part of that. Jesus thought of Sabbath as something made for us, a gift of God. Like some other Jewish teachers of his day, Jesus knew this gift could be poorly used, and he spoke up and took action when he saw such abuse. But Jesus honored the Sabbath. In the early years of the church when most Christians were Jews first, his followers did the same. But very early they also had the custom of gathering for the "breaking of the bread" on the first day of the week, the day of resurrection. Gradually, as there came to be many more non-Jewish converts to Christianity, it was this day, Sunday, that Christians began to think of as their Sabbath. Most often they called it simply "the Lord's day."

But this day was still about freedom, for the day of Christ's resurrection meant freedom from sin and from death and from slavery of every kind. And such freedom still needed to express itself, to take on flesh so that it could be heard and seen and felt and tasted in people's lives. At various times, Christians made some of the same mistakes with the Sabbath that Jesus had encountered, turning it into a day of rigid regulations rather than a celebration of freedom and a witness to the covenant between the Lord and creation.

Keeping the Sabbath Holy Today.

Today we encounter Sunday not so much as God's gift, or as a law about not working and going to church, but only as one day of the weekend when we somehow have to work the church service into a hectic schedule of leisure activities.

If we were to search now for Sunday as God's gift, a holy day, our long tradition could give us some help. There's the whole idea of a day of rest, a day to let things just be, a day of restoration when we don't pull creation, ourselves and each other apart, but let the wounds and work of six days heal. It helps to think of Sunday as a day to be whole: on other days I am worker, student, parent, spouse, cook, television-watcher, meeting-attender. On Sunday, I am just me.

An individual or a family pursuing such a Sunday would have to ease into it. Just a few hours at first, getting used to the idea of non-productive time, of time just to be, to sit and rock, or take a walk, or do whatever will gather the spirit that gets scattered throughout the long week.

Part of this is certainly a way to leave the cares and demands of the other six days behind. Sunday must be so filled with its own excitement, its own calm, too, and its own holiness and wholeness that we can find no place for business-as-usual. Ask: "What would have to happen for me to lay down those cares on Saturday evening and not return to them until Sunday night—or even Monday morning?" Ask: "What sort of a day would be good for my soul, my deepest self?" Specifics are bound to differ from one of us to another, but together we can perhaps shape a Sabbath.

Sunday Is Somebody!

Think of Sunday as a somebody, a person, a very special presence of the Lord. We know a little about how to think of the Lord as present in the blessing and breaking of bread and as present in the community, the holy communion. Our tradition, neglected though it is, tells us of this special presence also: the Lord present in time, in a day, in Sabbath.

That conviction is what gives Jewish observance of the Sabbath some of its most beautiful expression in prayer. The Sabbath is welcomed as a guest, indeed as a queen or a bride arriving in the home and in the soul. Its presence there is honored, celebrated, marked with delights, cherished with quiet and with study of the scripture. Finally, the home and the soul say farewell to this presence as the week returns.

In the pages that follow many prayers and rites are taken from the Jewish prayerbook for the Sabbath. They should be completely at home in a Christian household. But much depends on making a commitment not only to letting these rites for welcoming and leaving the Sabbath be a part of our household prayer, but to letting them really surround and embrace a whole day, a day when we "play kingdom." That is what our ancestors meant when they called our Sabbath "the eighth day," a day beyond time, a day like the coming reign of God.

Using This Section
The prayers for the Sunday-welcoming meal, the meal of Saturday evening, could be used without variation through the whole year. However, the various seasonal sections in this book do suggest some minor variations to fit each season.

The brief "Sunday Morning Prayer" would, on Sundays, replace the "Morning Prayer Together" found in the previous section.

"Scripture at Home" suggests that the scripture readings from the Sunday liturgy of the parish be studied in the home. The readings for all the Sundays of the year are given.

Finally, "Leavetaking" is a short Sunday evening prayer for marking the end of the holy day and the return of the week.

Even our first small ways to keep Sunday holy will begin to create an environment for our coming together to celebrate the eucharist. That gathering is to let the scriptures tell again some part of our story, to sing and reflect on the story and then to bless and share bread and wine as the holy communion. Such a special celebration of our congregation needs a setting, a surrounding in our lives. The ears and eyes, heart and mind and body, all need to make a space where the eucharist can happen. That is what keeping Sunday as a whole day does.

The prayers of Sunday are filled with gestures and things: eating from a special loaf of bread, sharing a cup of wine, lighting candles, smelling spices. These actions give shape, body, to that spirit we welcome on Sunday. Even if only one of them is done, with reverence and beauty, it can put us in touch with the holiness of this day.

The Sunday-welcoming Meal

This ritual may be used on Saturday evening to welcome the coming of Sunday, to mark Sunday as a holy day. Most of the prayers are taken from various Jewish rites for welcoming Sabbath; they have the beautiful sense of the holy day as a way in which God is present to the household and the community.

In preparation for this meal the table should be specially prepared. This might mean a fine tablecloth, good plates and silverware, cloth napkins, or whatever will make it festive and warm. At least two candles are on the table. Other lights are dimmed so that the candlelight may be seen and used.

On the table is a fine goblet or glass filled with wine. There may also be a special loaf of bread. The meal itself should be such that the preparation will not destroy the peace and festivity of the sabbath. It might even be quite simple, with perhaps some thing, such as homemade bread, to make it different from the other meals of the week.

Note that the word *Sabbath* is used throughout because Sunday has been the Christian Sabbath. You may wish to use the word Sunday instead.

All are standing at their places. In silence, one (traditionally, the mother) lights the candles and prays:
Come, let us welcome the Sabbath.
May its radiance illumine our hearts as we kindle these tapers.

Looking at the lights, all may pray silently for one another. Then the one who lighted the candles concludes:
May the Lord bless us with Sabbath joy.
May the Lord bless us with Sabbath holiness.
May the Lord bless us with Sabbath peace.

Parents and other adults place their hands in blessing on the heads of the children and one adult prays this blessing or some other, even a spontaneous blessing:

May the Lord bless you and keep you.

May the Lord make his face shine upon you and be kind to you.

May the Lord turn his face toward you and give you peace.

Then all are seated and a song of welcome to the Sabbath may be sung. The following traditional song of welcome may be used with any tune that fits the meter of the poem (for example, "Praise God From Whom All Blessings Flow").*

Let all rejoice with all their might,
The Sabbath freedom brings and light;
Let songs of praise to God ascend,
And voices sweet in chorus blend.

Now come, O blessed Sabbath-Bride,
Our joy, our comfort and our pride;
All cares and sorrow now bid cease,
And fill our waiting hearts with peace.

The leader of the prayer lifts up the cup of wine and prays:

Blessed are you, Lord, God of all creation,
Creator of the fruit of the vine.

Blessed are you, Lord, God of all creation,
you have taught us the way of holiness through your commandments
and have granted us your favor
and given us your holy Sabbath as an inheritance.
This day is a memorial of creation.
It is a memorial of the breaking of the bonds of slavery and sin and death.
Blessed are you, O Lord; you make holy the Sabbath day.

---

* Instead of the hymn "Let all rejoice . . ." the following could be sung to the simple melody of "Michael, row your boat ashore . . ."
  Welcome, welcome, day of rest, Alleluia!
  Day of joy the Lord has blessed. Alleluia!

The cup is then passed to everyone at the table. When all have taken a drink, the bread is held up and blessed.

Blessed are you, Lord, God of all creation;
you bring forth bread from the earth.

The bread is passed and shared and the meal is served.

After the meal, a special thanksgiving prayer may be recited; this psalm celebrates the Sabbath as a taste of the world to come, the heavenly Jerusalem to which we exiles return.

When the Lord brought back the captives of Zion,
   we were like men dreaming.
Then our mouth was filled with laughter,
   and our tongue with rejoicing.
Then they said among the nations,
   "The Lord has done great things for them."
The Lord has done great things for us;
   we are glad indeed.
Restore our fortunes, O Lord,
   like the torrents in the southern desert.
Those that sow in tears
   shall reap rejoicing.
Although they go forth weeping,
   carrying the seed to be sown,
They shall come back rejoicing,
   carrying their sheaves.

(Psalm 126)

The rest of the evening after this meal welcoming Sabbath would ideally be a very free time so that the joy and leisure of the meal could overflow into the night.

Sunday Morning Prayer

Since Sunday morning is usually kept with the celebration of the eucharist, only a brief ritual for the home is given here. Special psalms for Sunday mornings are given in the Advent, Lent and Eastertime sections.

To begin, all sing:
> On this day, the first of days,
> God the Father's name we praise;
> Who, creation's Lord and Spring,
> Did the world from darkness bring.

> On this day th'eternal Son
> Over death his triumph won;
> On this day the Spirit came
> With the gifts of living flame.

> God, the blessed Three in One,
> May thy holy will be done;
> In thy word our souls are free,
> And we rest this day with thee.

Then this psalm could be read by one or by all together:
> Sing joyfully to the Lord, all you lands;
>> serve the Lord with gladness;
>> come before him with joyful song.
> Know that the Lord is God;
>> he made us, his we are;
>> his people, the flock he tends.
> Enter his gates with thanksgiving,
>> his courts with praise;
> Give thanks to him; bless his name, for he is good:
>> the Lord, whose kindness endures forever,
>> and his faithfulness, to all generations.

(Psalm 100)

Scripture at Home

Every Sunday the church tells a part of its story. This is done at the liturgy through the reading of certain scriptures. The individual or the family may want to take this Sunday storytelling into the home: to have a way of preparing for the scriptures that will be heard and a way of letting them linger afterwards.

In Appendix I are given the scriptures for each Sunday of the year. On some Sundays the household can prepare for what they will be hearing at the liturgy, and on others can follow up the liturgy with another reading and perhaps some discussion and study of these passages. This study would not be so much like a classroom: rather, a probing of the scripture passage, reflecting, sharing, responding to what it tells us of ourselves. Sometimes, it would help to keep a little notebook for this scripture study, entering each week a short summary of the readings and a question or a reflection or a quote from the homily or a newspaper or a poem that the reading brings to mind.

The Sundays are listed in Appendix I with the titles given them in the Roman calendar for the church year. Except for a few variations this three-year cycle of scriptures is shared by Episcopal and Lutheran churches and increasingly in other Protestant denominations as well. The Sunday liturgy will ordinarily tell you where you are each week and where you will be next week. The Sundays called "Ordinary Time" or "Sundays of the Year" come between Epiphany and Lent and between Pentecost and Advent. Depending on the date of Easter, a varying number of these come before Lent.

The scripture readings for Sunday are planned on a three-year cycle. The new cycle begins each year with the first Sunday in Advent. In the coming years:

>Advent in 1979 begins Cycle C
>Advent in 1980 begins Cycle A
>Advent in 1981 begins Cycle B
>Advent in 1982 begins Cycle C

And so on. Thus, for example, all of 1979, until Advent, is Cycle B, and all of 1980, until Advent, is Cycle C. Note that on the third, fourth and fifth Sundays of Lent the readings of Cycle A may be chosen even in other years.

Leavetaking

This is a prayer for Sunday evening, a way of bidding farewell to the Sabbath guest. The prayers here are based on the Jewish Havdalah, the rite of "separation" which divides the Sabbath from the other days of the week. The family gathers around a cup of wine, a candle, and a small container of good-smelling spices.

A candle is lighted in silence; it may be given to one of the children to hold. One or several then pray by the light of the candle:

Behold, God is my deliverer!
　　I will trust in him and will not be afraid.
The Lord is my strength and song;
　　he is my deliverer.
The Lord alone is our help;
　　may he bless his people.
The Lord of the universe is with us;
　　the God of Jacob is our protection.
I will lift the cup of salvation
　　and call upon the name of the Lord.

One then holds up the wine cup:

Blessed are you, Lord, God of all creation;
　　you have given us the fruit of the vine.

All drink from the cup. Then one holds up the spices:

Our God, we thank you for the joy and rest of this day.
As we inhale the fragrance of the spices,
we pray that the days ahead may bring sweetness to our
　　lives
and to the lives of all your children.
May we yearn for the coming of your reign, the Sabbath
　　without end.
Blessed are you, Lord, God of all creation,
Creator of the spices.

The spices are passed and all inhale their fragrance. Then the candle is held high and one person prays:

Blessed are you, Lord, God of all creation,
Creator of the light of fire.
Blessed is the Lord,
who separated the Sabbath day from the other days.

Then the candle is extinguished. In the darkness, the leader prays:

The light is gone and Sabbath with it, but hope brightens the night for us.

Forgive our sins, O Lord, and let them be as yesterday when it is past.

Hear our prayer! Grant redemption!

In closing, everyone may sing "Shalom" or some other song of blessing.

Shalom, O my friends!
Shalom, O my friends!
Shalom, shalom!
Till we meet again,
till we meet again:
Shalom, shalom!

Chapter 3

✠✠✠

ADVENT

Introduction

December brings the shortest days of the year. More darkness. Little light from a sun that seems lost in the southern sky. But then—things turn around! Before December has gone the days are just a tiny bit longer. All over the northern parts of the earth, through ages and ages, peoples have held celebrations when the sun was reborn, when there was even a little more light. For even that much is all the promise that is needed.

That is really why we have Christmas on December 25. The people who became Christians in the first generations were used to a celebration at this time of year: a birthday party for the sun, earth's best friend. But Jesus was like that too, a sun, the light of the world. And so this solstice time became his birthday anniversary.

Advent is the way we keep these darkest days of the year as a preparation. Advent happens in the dark, and it is filled with our fears. Few of us ever really get over being scared of the dark, so this season lets us be the frightened folk that we are. It gathers all our fears—economic, political, social, family, health, death—into that one big fear of darkness.

Only frightened people can really keep Advent: "Be comforted!" "Don't be afraid!" Prophets and angels shout and sing through the Advent nights with that message. It is the hint of a promise. To keep Advent is to live by God's promises that are stronger than our fears.

The waiting is hard. It is also special. Advent is life's waitings now filled with the very beauty of time: waiting to be born, to grow, to give birth, to find friends, to die. "What a friend we have in time: gives us babies, makes us wine, tells us what to take and leave behind."

The prayers of Advent begin with the fourth Sunday before Christmas. It is a season that needs the protection of firm personal and family decisions about the ways it will be kept. Only an Advent of waiting, of simple prayer in its darkness, can bring us to the festival of Christmas.

Morning and evening prayers for Advent weekdays are given below. These are complete in themselves. Scripture readings for the weekdays are listed. The blessing of the advent wreath is included under "Advent Sundays" along with some special prayers to be used at the Sunday-welcoming meal and Sunday morning prayer. The Jewish festival of Hanukkah is then explained and some prayers are given for its observance. Finally, there are prayers for festivals of saints in early December, and a selection of Advent customs. The latter may help the family with children in making Advent a special time in itself rather than having it swallowed up by Christmas anticipation.

Advent Morning Prayer

The format for this prayer is the same as that in the "Daily Prayer" section. One psalm is given within the body of the prayer and an alternative is given at its conclusion. One of these should be selected and kept throughout the season so that it can become thoroughly familiar. Several possible songs are given, and since all are familiar, different ones could be sung from day to day.

Even though the prayer might frequently be used before sunrise, it would be appropriate to the season if it were prayed while standing and facing east.

Call to Prayer
As all make the sign of the cross:
Leader: The Lord shall come when morning dawns,
    All: And earth's dark night is past.

Song

(*1*) Wake, awake, for night is flying:
The watchmen on the heights are crying,
Awake, Jerusalem, arise!
Midnight's solemn hour is tolling,
His chariot wheels are nearer rolling,
He comes; O Church, lift up thine eyes!
Rise up, with willing feet
Go forth, the Bridegroom meet:
Hallelujah!
Lo, great and small, we answer all;
We follow where thy voice shall call.

(*Philip Nicolai*)

(*2*) *This song can be sung with its own tune, or the two verses can be combined and sung as one verse to the tune of "Sing of Mary."*
Hark! A thrilling voice is sounding!
"Christ is near," we hear it say,
"Cast away the works of darkness,
O you children of the day."

Wakened by the solemn warning,
Let the earth-bound soul arise;
Christ, her Sun, all sloth dispelling,
Shines upon the morning skies.

(*Saint Ambrose*)

(*3*) *This version of Psalm 24 can be sung to the tune of "When the Saints Go Marching In."*
Lift up your heads, you mighty gates!
Be lifted up, O ancient doors!
For the king of glory is coming,
He will rule for ever more!

The earth is his and all its lands,
And all the folk of every race!
For he has founded the hills and the oceans
And put the mountains in their places.

The Song of Zechariah: Luke 1:68–71, 76–79

"Blessed be the Lord the God of Israel
  because he has visited and ransomed his people.
He has raised a horn of saving strength for us
  in the house of David his servant,
As he promised through the mouths of his holy ones,
  the prophets of ancient times:
Salvation from our enemies
  and from the hands of all our foes.
And you, O child, shall be called
  prophet of the Most High;
For you shall go before the Lord
  to prepare straight paths for him,
Giving his people a knowledge of salvation
  in freedom from their sins,
All this is the work of the kindness of our God;
  he, the Dayspring, shall visit us in his mercy
To shine on those who sit in darkness and in the shadow of
    death,
  to guide our feet into the way of peace."

Scripture

If the scripture is to be read with morning prayer, the reference will be found in this chapter under "Scripture Readings for Advent Weekdays." All are seated for the reading and the silence.

Silence

Prayer

All stand; hands could be raised in a gesture of expectation.
Leader: We wait in joyful hope.
  All: For the coming of our Savior, Jesus Christ.
Leader: Lord our God, you are the fullness of dawn
      and we wait for you through the long darkness of
        night.
    We praise you for your promises,
      they are stars in our night time of fear;
      they are the quiet dawn in our night time of waiting.

This advent morning we give you praise for . . .
May all the hours of this new day bring nearer the
 fullness of time.
We watch and we pray in Jesus' name. Amen.

Doxology
This can be sung by all or read by the leader. All bow deeply.
 All praise, eternal Son, to thee
 Whose advent sets thy people;
 Whom with the Father we adore
 And Holy Ghost for evermore.
Leader: Come, Lord Jesus!
 All: Come quickly!

Alternate Psalm
Psalm 85:9–14
 I will hear what God proclaims;
  the Lord—for he proclaims peace.
 To his people, and to his faithful ones,
  and to those who put in him their hope.
 Near indeed is his salvation to those who fear him,
  glory dwelling in our land.
 Kindness and truth shall meet;
  justice and peace shall kiss.
 Truth shall spring out of the earth,
  and justice shall look down from heaven.
 The Lord himself will give his benefits;
  our land shall yield its increase.
 Justice shall walk before him,
  and salvation, along the way of his steps.

Advent Evening Prayer

With December's early darkness the evening prayer can often
be said after sunset. The prayer takes place around the Advent
wreath. The Bible, open to the scripture reading of the day,
might be placed beside the wreath. Artificial lights should be off
or very dim so that the candle light can be seen in its strength
and beauty. Lighting the Advent candles is a very special part of

this prayer and should be done by someone other than the leader. Children, if they take part, might take turns as candle lighters.

Call to Prayer
Standing or sitting around the wreath, all may make the sign of the cross:
Leader: Do not be afraid!
   All: Our God will come quickly, Alleluia!
Then the proper number of candles are lighted on the Advent wreath (one the first week, two the second, and so on).

Song
When the candles are burning, all sing one or more verses from "O Come, O Come, Emmanuel." A group may sing only the verse assigned below for a specific evening, or may sing all the verses up to and including the one for that evening. Note that the refrain ("Rejoice . . .") is not used until the last week of Advent.
From the first Sunday to the following Tuesday:
   O come, O Wisdom from on high,
   and order all things far and nigh;
   To us the path of knowledge show
   And cause us in her ways to go.
From Wednesday to Friday of the first week:
   O come, O come, O Lord of might,
   Who to your tribes on Sinai's height
   In ancient times bestowed the law
   In cloud and majesty and awe.
From Saturday of the first week to Tuesday of the second week:
   O come, O Rod of Jesse's stem,
   From ev'ry foe deliver them
   Who trust your mighty pow'r to save,
   And give them vict'ry o'er the grave.
From Wednesday to Friday in the second week:
   O Key of David, come once more,
   And open wide the heav'nly door;
   Make safe the way that leads on high,
   That we no more have cause to sigh.

From Saturday of the second week to Tuesday of the third week:
    O come, O Dayspring from on high,
    And cheer us by your drawing nigh;
    Disperse the gloomy clouds of night
    And death's dark shadow put to flight.
From Wednesday to Friday in the third week:
    O come, Desire of nations, bind
    All peoples in one heart and mind;
    Bid envy, strife and quarrels cease,
    And fill the world with heaven's peace.
From Saturday of the third week until December 23:
    O come, O come, Emmanuel,
    And ransom captive Israel
    That mourns in lonely exile here
    Until the Son of God appear.
        Rejoice, rejoice, O Israel!
        To you shall come Emmanuel.

Psalm 85:2–8

    You have favored, O Lord, your land;
        you have restored the well-being of Jacob.
    You have forgiven the guilt of your people;
        you have covered all their sins.
    You have withdrawn all your wrath;
        you have revoked your burning anger.
    Restore us, O God our savior,
        and abandon your displeasure against us.
    Will you be ever angry with us,
        prolonging your anger to all generations?
    Will you not instead give us life;
        and shall not your people rejoice in you?
    Show us, O Lord, your kindness,
        and grant us your salvation.

Scripture
The scripture for the day is read now; see "Scripture Readings for Advent Weekdays." All are seated until the Lord's Prayer.

Silence

Prayers of Intercession

Leader: In the quiet waiting of our advent, let us pray to the Lord.

Then anyone can speak short prayers of petition, sorrow, forgiveness, praise, thanksgiving. Each prayer is followed by a few moments of silence. In conclusion:

Leader: God of the promise, listen to our prayers.

Be with us through this night,

be close to us in our fears and in our hopes,

and bring us to the brightness of morning.

We ask this in the name of Jesus the Lord. Amen.

The Lord's Prayer

All stand and join hands to pray the Our Father.

Blessing

Leader: May God, whose mercy is from age to age,

who lifts up the oppressed and fills the hungry with good things,

turn toward us and give us peace.

All: Amen.

The prayer concludes here, but on occasion the candles could be put out and everyone remain in the darkness, in silence or conversation, for some minutes.

Scripture Readings for Advent Weekdays

Scripture selections for the weekdays of Advent will be found here. Readings for the Sundays of Advent are found in Appendix I.

First Week

M   Is 2:1–5, Mt 8:5–11

T   Is 11:1–10, Lk 10:21–24

W   Is 25:6–10, Mt 15:29–37

T   Is 26:1–6, Mt 7:21, 24–27

F   Is 29:17–24, Mt 9:27–31

S   Is 30:19–26, Mt 9:35—10:1, 6–8

Second Week
 M Is 34:1–10, Lk 5:17–26
 T Is 40:1–11, Mt 18:12–14
 W Is 40:25–31, Mt 11:28–30
 T Is 41:13–20, Mt 11:11–15
 F Is 48:17–19, Mt 11:16–19
 S Sir 48:1–4, 9–11, Mt 17:10–13

Third Week
 M Nm 24:2–7, 15–17, Mt 21:23–27
 T Zep 3:1–2, 9–13, Mt 21:28–32
 W Is 45:6–8, 18, 21–25, Lk 7:18–23
 T Is 54:1–10, Lk 7:24–30
 F Is 56:1–3, 6–8, Jn 5:33–36

The following replace the above readings when appropriate:
 Dec 17 Gn 49:2, 8–10, Mt 1:1–17
 18 Jer 23:5–8, Mt 1:18–24
 19 Jgs 13:2–7, 24–25, Lk 1:5–25
 20 Is 7:10–14, Lk 1:26–38
 21 Sg 2:8–14, Lk 1:39–45
 22 1 Sam 1:24–28, Lk 1:46–56
 23 Mal 23:1–4, 23–24, Lk 1:57–66

Advent Sundays

The Sundays of Advent, as of all the seasons, are first of all Sundays. They have their own specialness apart from the season. Yet they may take on something of the Advent mood: the candles of the Advent wreath could replace the usual Sabbath candles at the meal of Saturday night, the sound of Advent song might be heard instead of the usual song of Sunday, and the scriptures of each Advent Sunday can shape the prayer and reflection of that day.

The Advent Wreath

This is a circle of evergreen that grows brighter as we come closer to the birthday celebration of light itself, sun and son. It can be made in any number of ways. Usually the evergreen branches are bound to a frame. This can be a circle made of wire (coat hangers do well), wood, or styrofoam. If the wreath is to sit on a table, the candles can simply stand within: one the first week, two the second, three the third and, finally, four candles until Christmas. These too can be homemade or selected with care from a candleshop. The branches can be kept fresh by adding new ones occasionally.

The wreath is placed where it can remain throughout Advent: perhaps the spot where the crèche will be placed on Christmas Eve. This is the place where the household can gather for prayers each evening. The wreath first appears as the first Sunday of Advent is welcomed on Saturday evening. The new candles for each week are added on the following Saturday nights. Just before the first candle is lighted, the household may join in blessing the wreath. All extend their hands over the wreath as one prays:

Blessed are you, Lord, God of all creation,
for you have brought us to this season of waiting and of hope,
and have given us the darkness and the light.

The Sunday-welcoming Meal

Everything remains the same as on ordinary Sundays. However, the candles of the Advent wreath could be lighted as the Sabbath is welcomed. Instead of the usual song, a verse of "O Come, O Come, Emmanuel" could be sung. Like the other Sabbath hymns, this chant is an invitation, a longing, a welcoming.

The following blessing prayer could be used during Advent; it is spoken as the cup of wine is raised.

Blessed are you, Lord, God of all creation;
Creator of the fruit of the vine.

Blessed are you, Lord, God of all creation;
you have taught us the way of holiness through your commandments
and have granted us your favor
and given us your holy Sabbath as an inheritance.

This is a memorial of creation,
a memorial of the breaking of the bonds of slavery and sin
and death.
This day is a promise,
it is preparing the way,
it is the coming of the new creation.
Blessed are you, Lord, for you make holy the Sabbath day.
As usual, the wine is then passed to everyone at the table.

Sunday Morning Prayer

The usual prayer for Sunday morning (see "Sunday Morning Prayer," Chapter 2) is used, but Psalm 80 could be used instead of Psalm 100. The response, "Let your face shine and we shall be saved," would be learned by everyone so that it could be repeated each time the reader says: "Lord God of might, restore us!"

O Shepherd of Israel, hearken,
> O guide of the flock of Joseph!
From your throne upon the cherubim, shine forth
> before Ephraim, Benjamin and Manasseh.
Rouse your power,
> and come to save us.

Lord God of might, restore us!
All: Let your face shine and we shall be saved!

O Lord of hosts, how long will you burn with anger
> while your people pray?
You have fed them with the bread of tears,
> and given them tears to drink in ample measure.
You have left us to be fought over by our neighbors,
> and our enemies mock us.

Lord God of might, restore us!
All: Let your face shine and we shall be saved!

A vine from Egypt you transplanted;
> you drove away the nations and planted it.
You cleared the ground for it,
> and it took root and filled the land.

Why have you broken down its walls,
    so that every passer-by plucks its fruit?

Lord God of might, restore us!
All: Let your face shine and we shall be saved!

Look down from heaven and see;
    take care of this vine and protect what your right hand
      has planted.
May your help be with the man of your right hand,
    with the son of man whom you yourself made strong.
Then we will no more withdraw from you;
    give us new life, and we will call upon your name.

Lord God of might, restore us!
All: Let your face shine and we shall be saved.

Advent Meal Prayers

During Advent, the evening meal prayer could begin by sitting
for some moments in darkness and silence. Then the leader
strikes a match and lights a candle (or the appropriate number
of candles on the advent wreath if it is on the table).

    Leader: Come, Lord Jesus!
      All: Come quickly!

The prayer could then be a song or psalm from the evening
prayer for Advent, or this litany; all respond "Come, Lord!" to
each of the invocations spoken by the leader.

    Leader: O Wisdom
           O Lord of might
           O Root of Jesse
           O Key of David
           O Light of dawn
           O Desire of nations
           O Emmanuel

  Then one of the following prayers:
    Blessed be God in the darkness and in the light!
    Blessed be God in the promise and in the waiting!
    Blessed be God who like a shepherd feeds his flock!

Lord, bless us and the food we now share.
We wait for that time when the wolf shall be the guest of the
   lamb,
when the calf and the lion shall browse together,
when there shall be no more war or hurt on all your earth.

Hanukkah

Like Christmas, the Jewish winter festival of Hanukkah has its
origins in the change that happens to the sun, to the balance of
light and darkness. One legend, preserved in the Talmud, takes
the festival back to Adam:

> With the approach of the first winter, Adam began to see
> the days getting shorter. "Woe is me," he said, "because I
> must have sinned, and as a punishment the world around
> me is being darkened and returned to a state of chaos and
> confusion." So he fasted and prayed for eight days. How-
> ever, as he observed the winter solstice and noted the days
> getting increasingly longer, he said: "This is the way the
> world works." And he decided that from then on he would
> keep an annual eight-day festival.

And also like Christmas, Hanukkah has its historic occasion.
This is the victory of the Maccabees in the second century before Christ when their guerilla revolt drove out the foreign
occupiers of the land. Then the Maccabees rededicated the
temple. The word *Hanukkah* means "rededication."

The dual origins, in nature and in history, weave together in
the use of light. The legend says that when the temple was
recaptured, all of the sacred oil had been profaned except for a
tiny amount, enough to burn one day. But it took eight days to
sanctify new oil. A miracle then happened when the tiny bit of
oil burned the whole eight days. Thus the long nights of December, the approaching birthday of the sun, the lights of temple, the bright miracles of the Lord and the lights that are our
saints and heroes (our stars) give us a season and a ritual that is
among the most beautiful.

Many Christians like to observe Hanukkah because it celebrates so well what is part of our own heritage (the freedom won

by the Maccabees) and of universal heritage (the wonder of light and darkness). Hanukkah is dated by the moon and it lasts eight days. The simple ritual calls for only a menorah (the candleholder) and forty-four candles. Small birthday candles do well. One candle is lighted on the first night, two on the second night, and so on. Each night the "servant candle," the one used to light the others, also burns. Thus, the menorah needs a place for nine candles. A menorah can be specially purchased, or can be made from wooden spools, clay, tin, or anything that can be both simple and beautiful—and safe.

The first Hanukkah light is kindled on the evening before the first day of the festival. The date is determined by the lunar calendar. In coming years, the first day of Hanukkah will be:

> 1979 December 15
> 1980 December 3
> 1981 December 21
> 1982 December 11
> 1983 December 1

The prayer of Hanukkah should take place in darkness and candlelight. One candle, the servant candle, is lighted and held while this blessing is spoken:

Blessed are you, Lord, God of all creation,
for you have sanctified us with your commandments
and commanded us to kindle the light of Hanukkah.

Blessed are you, Lord, God of all creation,
for you performed miracles for our ancestors in those days
at this season.

On the first night only this blessing also:

Blessed are you, Lord, God of all creation,
for you have given us life and sustained us
and permitted us to reach this season.

Then the proper number of candles are lighted, and one or all may say:

We kindle these lights on account of the miracles, wonders
and deliverances
which you performed for our ancestors in those days at this
season.

These lights are sacred throughout the eight days of
  Hanukkah;
we are not permitted to make any use of them
but we are only to look at them,
in order to give thanks to you for your miracles, deliverances and wonders.

That concludes the prayers, except for sitting quietly and watch-
ing until the lights burn out. Songs known by heart could be
sung. The story of the Maccabees might be read or told at
sometime during the Hanukkah festival.

Saints' Days in Advent

These December festivals have the spirit of Advent. They make
a fine mosaic of the season. The prayers given here may be
added or substituted at the morning, evening or meal prayer
during Advent.

December 6—Saint Nicholas

Nicholas is a saint surrounded with stories. Most of these are
about his generosity and the wonders that sprang up all around
him. He is one of the mysterious gift-givers who hover around
the season, a remote ancestor of Santa Claus. Often he places
small gifts in shoes left just outside the door. Nicholas lived in
Asia about 300 years after Jesus.

Lord, you make this day special
with the memory of the good bishop Nicholas.
He praised you in all the wonders he worked,
he thanked you in all the gifts he shared with the poor.
May we have ears like Saint Nicholas to hear when any are
  in need,
and hands always ready to help and share.
Blessed are you, O Lord, in all your saints.

December 13—Saint Lucy or Santa Lucia

This is another ancient light and darkness festival, refashioned
in the Scandinavian countries for Lucia (whose name means
"light") with crowns of candles to brighten the very long winter

nights. Lucy lived about the same time as Nicholas; her home was Sicily, and the legends are of her martyrdom and of her great courage. These verses from Psalm 119 could be prayed with Saint Lucy today.

A lamp to my feet is your word,
    a light to my path.
I resolve and swear
    to keep your just ordinances.
I am very much afflicted;
    O Lord, give me life according to your word.
Accept, O Lord, the free homage of my mouth,
    and teach me your decrees.
Though constantly I take my life in my hands,
    yet I forget not your law.
The wicked have laid a snare for me,
    but from your precepts I have not strayed.
Your decrees are my inheritance forever,
    the joy of my heart they are.

Advent Customs and Rites

The Advent Calendar

This is a way to count down to Christmas. Each day of Advent has a door or a window to be opened and something new to look at. Many varieties of the Advent calendar are available in stores, but they can also be made at home:

1. Get out old Christmas cards. Cut out pictures and designs and people of all sizes, enough so that you have one for each day in Advent. Keep only one with Mary and Joseph and Jesus, the largest of all the pictures. Place all the pictures on a large piece of cardboard or heavy paper. The nativity picture is near the center. Paste all the pictures down.

2. Put another heavy piece of paper on top, covering everything. Cut its edges to be even with the cardboard underneath. The color of this paper should be quite light so that crayons and markers can be used to draw on it. Now cut flaps as windows, doors or other openings in the front paper over every picture.

Mark each of these openings with a small number for the date when that window will be opened. Begin with the first day of Advent and go up to December 24th ("24" goes on the door that opens to the nativity scene). Make sure that all the little openings close tightly.

3. Tape the covering sheet to the cardboard piece on all sides.
4. Now a picture can be drawn and colored on the top sheet, incorporating all the windows and doors.
5. Keep the calendar hanging by the breakfast table so that each door can be opened early in the day.

The Promises Branch

Advent is a season of promise. We come to know God's promise in the promises we make to one another.

Place a fallen branch, one with lots of little twigs on it, in a pail of sand. Put this at a place where the family can easily gather. Each day (or less often if you wish) one person makes a promise. Take turns. The promise is made by placing some sign for that promise on the branch, usually tying it on with thread. For example: a broom straw could mean a promise to sweep the floor, a spoon could be a promise to take the family out to eat. The person can tell the promise, keep it secret, or let everyone guess.

As Advent goes on, the branch becomes filled with our promises. On Christmas, it gives place to the Christmas tree.

Advent Friends

If the household is large, you can do this as one group, or a smaller group could join with other families.

Each one who wants to participate gets his/her name put into a hat. And each one draws a name out. Do this early in Advent. Nobody can tell whose name he/she has.

This name is your Advent friend. You are to find ways to do special things for that person. All kinds of surprises—but the person must never know who is responsible.

On Christmas or Epiphany try to guess who was whose Advent friend. Then tell!

Blessing of the Christmas Tree

Christmas trees should be decorated with an abundance of care and plenty of time. The histories of the ornaments need to be told. Finally, let the household surround the tree. Everyone places hands on the tree while one prays:

> God of all creation,
> may the ever-greenness of this tree
> bring life and hope to this home.
> We wait together for the coming of the Christ,
> the days of everlasting justice and peace.

Blessing of the Crêche

On Christmas Eve the crêche can be put in place, or completed, as the whole family joins in telling the story or reading it from the Gospel of Luke. When all the figures are in place, candles are lighted all around.

> God of Mary, Joseph, shepherds and animals,
> God of our advent promises,
> bless this crêche we have prepared
> in remembrance of the birth of your Son, Jesus.
> Fill all of us with the light of this holy night.

And then, finally, the first Christmas carols.

Chapter 4

✤✤✤

CHRISTMASTIME

Introduction

Christmas is a festival, a day when business-as-usual stops, a time when time itself can be forgotten. Festivals are made by people who are convinced that living deserves rejoicing. To be festive is to get out of the ordinary—but only because you know the secret of the ordinary. Festivals happen when the time comes round to tell the most special stories, and the story of Christmas is of a birth, that most out-of-the-ordinary ordinary event. If that story of the birth tells us a lot about who we are, then there is a chance we can make Christmas a true festival.

The power of this story and its festival is in its universality: to tell of a birth in this way is to touch a thousand thoughts in every human soul. It stirs deep feelings for that "wonderful exchange," that affirmation of God's promise, that sense of a possible end to our aloneness, that awe that God first loved us. But the festival must tell the story well. And we must be attentive to the story and not only to the embellishments.

It is this story of a birth that would have us leave behind the world of work and worry and enter into another kind of time, affirming a future that is uncontrolled by the past, acting as if the exile were over. The task now is freeing this story from its burdens of sentimentality, commercialism, associations with hectic and expensive days.

How to do that! It might help to savor some of the images

that poets have found for speaking of this story; they have a way
of tearing down façades that separate us from the story's power.
Consider:

> He cam also stille
>> Ther his moder was,
> As dew in Aprille
> That fallith on the gras.
>> *(15th century, anonymous)*

And another image:

> In time it came round, the time
> ripe for the birth of a boy.
> Much as a bridegroom steps
> fresh from the chamber of joy,
> arm in arm he arrived
> entwining the sweetheart he chose.
>> *(Saint John of the Cross, translated by John Nims)*

> "Into this bitter world, O Terrible Huntsman!"
> I say, and she takes my hand—"Hush,
> You will wake Him."
>> *(Kenneth Patchen)*

Or think for awhile about the verbs in this story, in this Christmas festival. List them. For starters: born, brought forth, dwelled,
joined, emptied, made flesh, loved.

Then ask: Does the Christmas festival we keep express these
actions? Are our rites and customs about getting born, taking
flesh, loving, dwelling, bringing forth?

And how long is this festival? Is it over Christmas morning?
Our tradition is that it takes from Christmas to Epiphany to tell
this story and keep its festival. If Advent runs right up to
Christmas Eve, then we have a chance. To help keep the whole
season, this section contains a form for daily prayer during
Christmastime, special meal blessings, and prayers for the most
special days in the twelve days of Christmas.

Meal Prayers at Christmas

The stuff of which this blessing is made is the love that went into the selection and preparation of the food, the generosity of those who labored that such food might be purchased, the beauty of the table which has been set, the special leisure which makes fellowship at table possible. The blessing begins when all have assembled at the table. The ringing of some jingle bells or sleigh bells might call everyone to silence. Then, still in silence, the oldest child lights the candles on the table. When they are burning, one of the adults (perhaps the oldest one present) prays:

> For the wonder of birth, we thank you, Lord.
> And for this day to celebrate the birth of Jesus at Bethlehem,
> the house of bread.
> We sing then with the angels,
> with the cattle and the sheep,
> with the shepherds and the stars of heaven,
> with Joseph and Mary:

(*Here all join hands and sing:*)
> O come let us adore him!
> O come let us adore him!
> O come let us adore him, Christ the Lord.

(*Then the leader continues as all take up their wine glasses and hold them as for a toast:*)
> May your blessing, O God, be upon all creation.
> May the earth that brought forth this food be blessed,
> and all the hands that have prepared it.
> May this food be blessed by you and by all of us
> and so become the first banquet of this holy season.
> May our sharing of this meal be like the sharing at Bethlehem
> when in Jesus we had a part in your own holiness.

(*Then all say a "Merry Christmas!" and drink together.*)

This blessing can be used for festive meals all through the Christmastime. Simply add, in the first prayer:

On Holy Family:
>. . . the birth of Jesus at Bethlehem, the house of bread, into the holy family of Joseph and Mary.
>We sing then . . .

On Saint Stephen's Day:
>. . . the birth of Jesus at Bethlehem, the house of bread, and Stephen, the deacon, who was today born in heaven.
>We sing then . . .

On Saint John's Day:
>. . . and the holiness of his good friend John the Apostle.

On Holy Innocents:
>. . . and the holy innocent children of Bethlehem, victims of power and of cruelty.

On January 1:
>. . . the birth of Jesus at Bethlehem, the house of bread.
>Beginning this new year, we sing with the angels . . .

On Epiphany:
>. . . the birth of Jesus at Bethlehem
>and his manifestation to the Magi, to John in the Jordan, in the water-made-wine at the wedding, and to us.
>We sing then . . .

Different carols may be sung on different days. In the second prayer, the line that includes ". . . the first banquet . . ." is changed to:

>May this food be blessed by you and by all of us
>and so become a festive meal for this holy season.

At simple meals during Christmastime, the blessing might be a carol sung together.

Daily Prayer

Only one form of daily prayer is given here. Since the days of Christmastime, from December 25 to Epiphany (now usually celebrated on the Sunday after New Year's Day), are likely to be unusual ones, the household prayer may never be at the same time two days in a row. So these prayers are for morning or evening or whenever the family can gather. The place for the prayer could be around the tree or the crèche. Perhaps some bells might be on hand to ring during the singing. If the room is dark, candles are lighted around the crèche. Everyone is seated to begin. The leader selects one of the songs to be sung; other carols can be used.

Call to Prayer
Leader: Glory to God in the highest!
   All: And peace to his people on earth!

Song
Bells could be gently rung during any of these songs:
(1) Silent night, holy night!
     All is calm, all is bright
     Round yon virgin-mother and child.
     Holy infant so tender and mild,
     Sleep in heavenly peace,
     Sleep in heavenly peace.

     Silent night, holy night!
     Shepherds quake at the sight;
     Glories stream from heaven afar,
     Heav'nly hosts sing "Alleluia!"
     Christ, the Savior, is born!
     Christ, the Savior, is born!

(Joseph Mohr)

(2) Go, tell it on the mountain,
     Over the hills and ev'rywhere;
     Go, tell it on the mountain
     That Jesus Christ is born!

     While shepherds kept their watching
     O'er silent flocks by night,
     Behold throughout the heavens
     There shone a holy light. *(refrain)*

Down in a lowly manger
The humble Christ was born,
And God sent us salvation
That blessed Christmas morn. (*refrain*)

(3) Mary had a baby, Aye, Lord,
Mary had a baby, Aye, my Lord,
Mary had a baby, Aye, Lord,
The people keep a-coming and the train done gone.

What did she name him? Aye, Lord . . .

Named him Jesus. Aye, Lord . . .

(4) Yea, Lord, we greet thee,
Born this happy morning;
Jesus, to thee be
All glory giv'n;
Word of the Father,
Now in flesh appearing.

O come, let us adore him . . .

(*John Francis Wade*)

Canticle: Isaiah 9:1-6

The people who walked in darkness
    have seen a great light;
Upon those who dwelt in a land of gloom
    a light has shone.
You have brought them abundant joy
    and great rejoicing,
As they rejoice before you as at the harvest,
    as men make merry when dividing spoils.
For the yoke that burdened them,
    the pole on their shoulder,
And the rod of their taskmaster
    you have smashed, as on the day of Midian.
For every boot that trampled in battle,
    every cloak rolled in blood,
    will be burned as fuel for flames.

For a child is born to us, a son is given us;
upon his shoulder dominion rests.
They name him Wonder-Counselor, God-Hero,
Father-Forever, Prince of Peace.
His dominion is vast
and forever peaceful.

Scripture
These scriptures can be used on the various days of
Christmastime:
December 25: John 1:1–14
Sunday after Christmas (Holy Family): Luke 2:15–18
December 26, Saint Stephen: Acts 5:55–60
December 27, John the Apostle: Revelation 1:9–18
December 28, The Holy Innocents: Matthew 2:13–18
December 29: Isaiah 62:10–12
December 30: Isaiah 52:7–10
December 31: Numbers 6:22–27
January 1, Mary, Mother of God or Name Day: Luke
2:16–21
Epiphany (Sunday after New Year's): Matthew 2:1–12
Days between New Year's and Epiphany: Isaiah 60:1–6,
Isaiah 60:7–15, Isaiah 60:16–22, Ephesians 1:3–6, 15–18
When the Baptism of the Lord is celebrated on the Sunday after
Epiphany, the following readings are used on the week days
between the two feasts:
1 Jn 3:22–24, 1 Jn 4:7–10, 1 Jn 4:11–18, 1 Jn 4:19—5:4,
1 Jn 5:5–13, 1 Jn 5:14–21

Silence

Prayer
All stand and join hands.
Leader: The Word was made flesh, Alleluia!
All: And dwelt among us, Alleluia!

Then the following prayer is recited. Or the blessing below may be recited instead.

> We have listened to your word, O God.
> May we celebrate your presence with us in the birthday of Jesus.
> Through the wonder of that birth we seek you, Lord, in . . .

(Mention here particulars: areas where the family finds the hope of Christmas.)

> All through this day of Christmastime keep us in your care, and protect us in the quiet of the night.
> We ask this in the name of Jesus the Lord. Amen.

Blessing

Almighty God has chased away the darkness of the world
by the coming of the Messiah,
and has filled these nights and days with the light of Jesus' birth.
May God bless us and chase far away from us the darkness of sin,
and fill our hearts with the light of virtue.
Leader: Glory to God in the highest!
   All: And peace to his people on earth!

Feast Days During Christmastime

Holy Family

The Sunday after Christmas (unless Christmas is a Sunday it-self) is the Feast of the Holy Family. It might be a day when the family (whatever combination of people that is) has a tradition of doing something together, something adventurous.

As part of the Christmastime prayer, the following could be used today:

> God, our father and our mother,
> we thank you for the family of Joseph and Mary.
> It was at home with his parents that Jesus grew
> in wisdom and age and your grace,

that he learned to know the law and the prophets
and to do right and to love goodness.
Bless with strength and patience and good humor
all who would make such homes today.
We ask this in the name of Jesus the Lord. Amen.

This would be a good day for parents to begin to bless their children at bedtime, perhaps with a hand on the head or by making a sign of the cross on the child's forehead or heart. Words of blessing could be used also. For example:

May God bless you and keep you safe.
(or) May God smile on you and be kind to you.
(or) May God keep you in peace this night.

December 26—Saint Stephen's Day

Stephen was a deacon in the very early years of the church in Jerusalem. He was the first follower of Jesus to die as a martyr.

We have these three special days huddled around Christmas: Stephen, John and Holy Innocents. They seem to tell us: we cannot celebrate this birth without remembering that with every birth there is pain. Jesus used this image: "A woman in labor is in pain because her time has come . . ." It is an end for her, for her child, to one kind of life. It is a death. These two poles of human life are never that far apart. In his poem "Journey of the Magi," T. S. Eliot has one of the Magi reflect: "this Birth was/ Hard and bitter agony for us, like Death, our death." Perhaps that is why Christians have mixed the memories of so many wonderful and awesome and terrible things in these days of the birthday celebration of Jesus.

At prayer today, sing about what Good King Wenceslaus did on this day, and use the following:

Father, yesterday the Lord was born on earth
that today Stephen might be born in heaven.
Fill your church with Stephen's eagerness;
may we celebrate his birthday in heaven, as he did,
with forgiveness and delight.
We ask this in the name of Jesus the Lord. Amen.

December 27—Saint John's Day

John is called "the disciple Jesus loved." He was one of the first persons whom Jesus called. He was along with Peter and James for the Transfiguration; he went into the garden with Jesus the night before Jesus died. John was with Mary at the cross and he outran Peter to get to the empty tomb. He is said to have traveled to Rome where he kept his cool in boiling oil; another legend has him drinking poisoned wine without being harmed. His last years were spent on an island in exile. The fourth gospel and several epistles bear his name.

By tradition, this is the day to bless wine, perhaps because of that poisoned wine that did John no harm. One way to do this would be to fill a large, beautiful cup brimful. Leave the wine bottles on the table also. One person lifts the cup high and says:

> Blessed are you, Lord, God of all creation,
> for you have given us the fruit of the vine.

Then the cup is passed around the table, each person drinking and handing the cup on with a wish for the good health of the next person. A prayer for this day:

> Lord Jesus, in John you found a good friend,
> also a fisherman, a preacher, a poet,
> someone to love your mother as you loved her.
> On this festival of the apostle John,
> bless us with the time and patience to make friends
> and to be friends. Amen.

December 28—Holy Innocents Day

Again death is placed here side by side with birth. The story of the innocents is found in Matthew 2:16–18. And why such a story just three days after Christmas? Perhaps the festivity of this season was the only human way to sustain faith in the goodness of people and of God in the face of human atrocity. At any other time such stories of our cruelty to one another might make faith and the world seem absurd.

For the story of the killing of the innocent continues. Sometimes it comes close to home: Wounded Knee happened on

December 29 in 1890 in South Dakota. Each August we remember the innocents of Hiroshima and Nagasaki who died in
the atomic blasts of 1945. On the 27th of Nisan (a spring month
in the Jewish calendar) there is time for remembering the six
million Jews murdered in the concentration camps of World
War II. And since 1972 we need to remember the cruel bomb-
ing which the United States government inflicted that year's
Christmastime on the people of North Vietnam.

Why keep such memories alive? Because something of
Herod, of Indian-hating, of anti-Semitism lives on in us. We
need to remember. The hope and beauty of Christmas give us
the strength.

An eyewitness to the Wounded Knee massacre wrote:

> Men and women and children were heaped and scattered
> all over the flat at the bottom of the little hill where the
> soldiers had their wagonguns, and westward up the dry
> gulch all the way to the high ridge, the dead women and
> children and babies were scattered. . . . It was a good
> winter day when all this happened. The sun was shining.
> But after the soldiers marched away from their dirty work,
> a heavy snow began to fall. The wind came up in the night.
> There was a big blizzard, and it grew very cold. The snow
> drifted deep in the crooked gulch, and it was one long
> grave of butchered women, children and babies, who had
> never done any harm and were only trying to run
> away.   (*Black Elk Speaks,* edited by John G. Neihardt)

The following prayer could be used today. It is taken from
the Jewish prayerbook and was written and dedicated to those
who perished in World War II concentration camps, but it is
appropriate to this day when we remember the innocent Jewish
children of Bethlehem.

> At this hour of memorial we recall with loving reverence
> all of thy children who have perished through the cruelty
>   of the oppressor.
> Not punished for any individual guilt, but without dis-
>   crimination,

the aged and the young, the learned and the simple
were driven in multitudes along the road of pain and piti-
   less death.
Their very presence on earth was begrudged
for they brought to the mind of man
the recollection of thy covenant of mercy and justice. . . .
They have died, as did the martyrs of bygone days,
for the sanctification of thy Name on earth.

December 31–New Year's Eve

The bells that ring through the Christmastime are especially
needed tonight to ring out the old and to ring in the new. After
all, we are carrying on with the celebration of a birth, a beginning. Such a festival means that the future has all kinds of wild
possibilities. Let the midnight hour tonight bring the thrill that
goes with starting over.

> Lord, may we pass through the coming year with faithful
>   hearts.
> Then, in all things we shall please your loving eyes.
> We ask this in the name of Jesus the Lord. Amen.

This song, by Alfred Tennyson, could be used tonight also. It
works with any tune like "Praise God From Whom All Blessings
Flow."

> Ring out the old, ring in the new,
> Ring, happy bells, across the snow!
> The year is going, let him go;
> Ring out the false, ring in the true.
>
> Ring out the grief that saps the mind,
> For those that here we see no more;
> Ring out the feud of rich and poor;
> Ring in redress to all mankind.

January 1–Mary, Mother of God or Name Day

The story of Christmas continues with a moment of marveling
at Mary who had so many things to keep in her heart, and at
how she and Joseph took the child to be circumcised on the

eighth day and gave him the name Jesus. The prayers for today would be those for Christmastime, but the following could be used.

Leader: Blessed are you among women.

   All: And blessed is the fruit of your womb.

Song

Sing of Mary, pure and lowly,
Virgin-mother undefiled,
Sing of God's own Son most holy,
Who became her little child.
Fairest child of fairest mother,
God the Lord who came to earth,
Word made flesh, our very brother,
Takes our nature by his birth.

Prayer

Father,
source of light in every age,
the virgin conceived and bore your Son
who is called Wonderful God, Prince of Peace.
May her prayer, the gift of a mother's love,
be your people's joy through all ages.
May her response, born of a humble heart,
draw your Spirit to rest on your people.
We ask this in the name of Jesus the Lord. Amen.

A New Year's Day custom that deserves new revival is that of setting aside this day to visit friends: old friends and new, announced and unannounced visits. Nuts and seeds, symbolic of new life in the New Year, could provide the refreshments for the visiting.

Epiphany

January 6 is traditionally the feast of Epiphany, the end of the twelve days of Christmas. Like December 25, this date had ancient associations with the winter solstice; it is, in some places, kept as a birthday festival of the Lord. In several countries,

Epiphany is now kept on the Sunday which falls after New Year's Day.

Epiphany concludes the Christmas festival. In our final celebration we take down the tree and decorations, the crêche, the cards. The house is back to normal. But normal, for the house and the family, is not "the same as before"—not if the festival has been kept with heart and soul and body. Those who come out of a festival are not quite those who went in.

Epiphany is a bit of what Christmas could mean. It begins in the simple truth that to be born is to be seen. The Lord, taking flesh, was seen, was manifest. "Manifest" is what "epiphany" means. All the senses could discover the Lord. It is a day of excitement in which the church sometimes scrambles stories of how that manifesting happened. This is an adaptation of an ancient Epiphany verse that lets the manifestations of the Lord run together in one chaotic, joyous story:

> The Magi are coming!
> They're coming to a wonderful wedding
> where the guests are drinking water-turned-to-wine
> in celebration of the baptism of Jesus by John
> when the heavens were opened
> and everyone heard the proclamation that God dwells in
>   our flesh.

Epiphany Cake

This is one way to celebrate this day, year after year. It is your favorite beautiful high cake, covered with icing, and decorated with candles and candy to look like the crown of one of the Magi. In the cake have been placed three beans (or any number, depending on how large the family—the scripture never does say how many Magi there were). Crowns are made during the day, and old robes and gowns assembled. Those discovering beans in their pieces of cake are then crowned and vested and they preside over games and songs and storytelling and a grand procession through the house. This last can include the Epiphany blessing of the home.

Home Blessing on Epiphany

Epiphany is traditionally the day when homes are blessed. This could be done with a grand procession through every room. Everyone involved may have something to carry: candles, incense, the cross or crucifix, the symbols of the three Magi (gold, incense, myrrh). In each room one person asks the blessing. For example: "May this room be blessed in the name of the Father and of the Son and of the Holy Spirit."

Then holy water may be sprinkled, the whole room honored with incense, and anyone can wish a blessing on what happens in that room: "May this basement stay dry and cool!" "May this kitchen be fragrant for all who work here!" "May this bedroom be filled with sweet rest and good dreams!"

Sometimes it is customary to carry chalk and mark some of the doors with the year and the initials of the Magi (Casper, Melchior and Balthasar, according to the tradition). Crosses separate the letters and numbers: 19 † C † M † B † 79

At the end, a prayer and a party:

> Visit this home, we ask you, O Lord.
> Chase far away from it all the snares of the enemy.
> Send your holy angels to live with us and keep us at peace.
> May your blessing be always upon us. Amen.

Prayer on Epiphany

> Everlasting God, you are the brightness of faithful souls.
> You brought the nations to your light
> and made known to them the one who is the true light,
> the bright and morning star.
> Fill this world with your glory
> and show yourself by the radiance of your light into all
> nations.
> We ask this in the name of Jesus the Lord. Amen.

Chapter 5

✠✠✠

LENT

Introduction

Lent begins with Easter. The forty days exist only because of the "day that the Lord has made." The roots go very deep, in history and in each person. It is the springtime-coming (the English word "Lent" comes from a word for springtime). It is a return of life to the earth and a promise of life to the people of earth: flesh and blood have a future, body and spirit will be one for another year because there is warmth and rain again in the earth. It is that basic.

When people's lives were dictated by the climate, the end of winter meant a scarcity of provisions. What meat remained, frozen or salted, was in danger of spoiling with the occasional warm days. Rather than that, people held festivals to consume at one happy time all that was left of the meal. The word *carnival* originally applied to this end-of-winter holiday; it means "Good-bye to the meat." And with the meat gone and other provisions dwindling, there were some hard days ahead. Fasting wasn't invented by Jews and Christians.

But such very early springtime ways did help Christians to gradually define for themselves a season before the Easter-Passover celebration. In the centuries when the church was taking shape, each Easter marked the baptism of new Christians. Baptism ended years of preparation—not so much by studying books but of learning how to live in the faith witnessed by those already baptized. Each Lent the community took the candidate through the final stages of preparation: exorcisms, scrutinies and fasting and praying together. This ministry also reminded the community by the presence of these candidates of its own calling to life in Christ. The final weeks of preparation, which gradually became a period of forty days, were for all a time of renewal, an annual challenge to live the Gospel as fully as possible. The whole setting was right: the struggle of death and life in the earth inspired and reflected that struggle as it went on in the life of each candidate, as well as those already baptized, and in the very life of the community itself. And all of this was caught up, not only in the passion of Jesus, the events of his last hours, but in his entire ministry understood as a making present of the reign of God.

The keeping of Lent remains a Christian community's best hope of staying in touch with its roots and its visions. For its roots and visions are most clearly found in the way it initiates new members. For those of us already baptized, Lent is a rather dramatic summons to keep in mind who we are, what we have affirmed about God and Christ and Spirit, about church and our life together, about what is happening through every part of earth. Lent brings belief out of the abstract and puts it all in terms of us: our fasting, our prayer, our sharing. Lent retells the best stories we have; it doesn't even pretend these were long ago and far away. They are today, yesterday and tomorrow under this very roof.

What Christians have found about Lent is this: once we mark it with the practices and disciplines and rituals and prayers that are strong enough to serve the initiation of new Christians and the renewal of those already Christians, once we do this to make Lent year after year then somehow Lent becomes a kind of home for us. We there learn to be ourselves. The season identifies us, names us, tells us who we are and what we are about.

The forty days then need some time of preparation. By Ash Wednesday an individual or a family must already have given thought to the keeping of Lent. In particular, the lenten disciplines must be chosen, some for the individual and some for the family. These disciplines have often been considered under the three headings: prayer, fasting and almsgiving.

Prayer

The prayer of Lent might be fidelity to the morning and evening prayers which are given on the following pages. Or it might be daily prayers such as the rosary, or quiet meditation, or the stations of the cross. It might be at home, in the church building, or outside in the winter-turning-to-spring. The quality of the time for prayer is more important than the quantity: to choose some of the best moments of each day, to be fairly regular. Alone or together in prayer, silent time is especially fitting during Lent. Often this can be focused simply on one word from a scripture reading or a prayer; then that word can be allowed to pass again and again through the mind in a relaxed, leisurely way. It gets to be at home there.

Daily reading from the scriptures can also be part of the lenten prayer. The readings can be chosen from the ones assigned to each day in Lent or, for private reading especially, one might choose simply to read various books of the Bible. Especially appropriate to Lent would be Genesis, Exodus, Deuteronomy, Jeremiah, Ezekiel, Hosea, Jonah, the four gospels, and the Psalms.

Reading from other sources can also supplement the prayer of Lent. A book selected for private reading, or for reading aloud with the family, need not be explicitly religious. Consider novels, biography, poetry, or any writing that gives one much to reflect about. It may even be good to keep at hand a book of blank pages and out of the reading or the prayer or just the experiences of each day in Lent to write something in this book: a journal or diary entry, a short prayer, thoughts on the day's scripture or other reading.

Fasting

There are many ways to fast, to practice restraint, to enter fully into the winter-like death of Lent out of which there is incredible new life. Recent church tradition called for taking only one regular meal a day during Lent, with one or two very small meals and no food in between. That was both good discipline, a way of sharing the world's food resources, and a practice of appreciation for the wonder of food. Other kinds of restraint may also be fitting, though perhaps no one of them has all the qualities of this simple fasting. Some examples: doing without sugar, alcohol, drugs, or tobacco; abstaining from some sleep; doing without angry responses, impatience or other things that hinder us; limiting television; living one day a week on a poverty budget. Today most people are especially conscious of world hunger and what a complicated problem it is. The kinds of food we eat, as well as the amounts, serve to keep the problem before us and, even in small ways, we are learning to share the food we have. Abstaining from meat and depending for our nourishment on less wasteful ways of producing protein is good discipline in Lent or at any time.

Alms

First of all, the money which is saved by some form of fasting can be given where it is needed for food for the hungry of the community or the world. The gathering of this money, and whatever else members of the family wish to share, can be done in a plate which is placed on the table each day at dinnertime. A place can be set with this plate just as for anyone else in the family. Thus, if there are five persons in the family, six places are set during Lent and, at the sixth, is the plate for alms. This can be a very real reminder that we do not sit down to eat alone but that our table is part of the world's dining table, and the hungry of the world sit with us.

Alms are also given through efforts to share; spring cleaning is really a lenten custom, a way of recycling whatever is no longer in use. Sharing also happens with energy: deciding to walk instead of drive, keeping the home cooler, using containers which can be recycled. Time also is something that can be shared through visiting friends, persons in hospitals or rest homes or those confined to their own homes, persons in jail.

Usually it is a good idea for lenten promises to be written down and kept at the place of daily prayer throughout the season. On Easter they can be burned with the new fire.

The following pages contain prayers for the last day before Lent, for Ash Wednesday, the daily morning and evening prayers of Lent, some lenten elements for the customary Sunday prayer, lenten meal prayers, stations of the cross for use at home or in the church building, special prayers for Holy Week, and complete notes on the celebration of the Passover with the seder meal.

Tuesday Before Ash Wednesday

By ancient custom in the Western church, the alleluia is not spoken or sung during Lent. This absence of our most familiar acclamation or cheer is a simple but strong way of noting that these days are different.

At one time it was customary in some places for Christians to bury the alleluia before Lent. It could be done again, within the family, as a way to celebrate Mardi Gras, Fat Tuesday, the day before the lenten practices begin. With a spade, an empty wooden box, a beautiful "Alleluia!" drawn and colored on paper, and perhaps even with candles and incense, the family can have a procession to some garden spot, where a little grave can be dug. Then, after singing a last alleluia, the paper can be placed in the box, a top nailed on, and the "coffin" placed in the ground. In silence, everyone can help pile the dirt in the hole. Such a ritual, together with prayer for a good Lent, could come before or after a little Mardi Gras feasting.

This hymn was written to accompany the farewell to the alleluia; the tune would be that of a "Tantum Ergo" or any tune of that meter:

> Alleluia, sing of gladness,
> Voice of joy that cannot die;
> Alleluia is the anthem
> Ever dear to choirs on high;
> In the house of God abiding
> Thus they sing eternally.
>
> Alleluia, we deserve not
> Here to chant for evermore;
> Alleluia our transgressions
> Make us for a while give o'er;
> For the holy time is coming
> Biding us our sins deplore.

Therefore in our hymns we pray thee,
Grant us, blessed Trinity,
At the last to keep thine Easter
In our home beyond the sky;
There to thee forever singing
Alleluia joyfully.

A simpler farewell to the alleluia could be this: singing a favorite alleluia at the Tuesday evening meal, then this prayer:

We thank you, O Lord, for the alleluia,
our shout of joy, our song of gladness.
May we walk with Jesus through the forty days of this Lent
and so at Easter be new in his Spirit.
Then we shall sing as never before our alleluia.

And then a final alleluia is sung.

Ash Wednesday

This is the solemn beginning of the forty days. The day is marked with special fasting and prayer and ashes. If some members of the household cannot receive ashes at the church service, the family could be marked with the ashes at home. Have ready a scissors, a small glass bowl, and some wooden matches. The prayers below could also be used without the marking with ashes.

A bit of hair is cut from each person's head and this hair is placed in the glass bowl. All then kneel in silence as the hair is burned to ashes. Then:

Leader: Come back to the Lord with all your heart;
        leave the past in ashes
        and turn to God with tears and fasting
        for God is slow to anger and ready to forgive.

(Based on Joel 2:12–13)

Then all extend hands over the ashes in blessing and one says:

Lord,
bless these ashes
by which we show that we are dust.

Pardon our sins
and keep us faithful to the discipline of Lent,
    for you do not want sinners to die
    but to live with the risen Christ,
    who reigns with you for ever and ever. Amen.

When the ashes are cool, the oldest person takes some and either sprinkles them on the head of the next oldest or marks that person's forehead. The ashes could be sprinkled or marked in the sign of the cross. The one doing this says:

> Remember, (man or woman or child), that you are dust and to dust you will return.
> (*or*)
> Turn away from sin and be faithful to the gospel.
> (*or*)
> Keep Lent and be faithful to the gospel.

The one marked then marks the next person and so on until the youngest has given ashes to the oldest.

Conclude with one of the songs from the morning or evening prayer for Lent.

Lenten Morning Prayer

For morning prayer, gather at the usual place or at the cross, perhaps one that is hung especially for Lent. The leader selects which song will be sung each day. One psalm is given within the service and others, as options, immediately following. Ordinarily, one would be chosen and kept throughout the season. Each person will need to make a copy of the psalm until it is memorized.

All kneel throughout, except during the reading of scripture if this is done at morning prayer.

Call to Prayer
All make the sign of the cross.
Leader: This is the favorable time!
    All: This is the day of salvation!

Song

(1) To the tune of "Michael, Row Your Boat Ashore"; additional verses can be made up:

> In our Lent we fast and pray; Lord, have mercy.
> Jesus, help us start this day. Lord, have mercy.
>
> Forty days we struggle, Lord; Lord, have mercy.
> Springtime brings a great reward. Lord, have mercy.
>
> Praise the Father, praise the Son; Lord, have mercy.
> Praise the Spirit, God is one. Lord, have mercy.

(2)   Jesus walked this lonesome valley;
> He had to walk it by himself.
> O, nobody else could walk it for him;
> He had to walk it by himself.
>
> We must walk this lonesome valley . . .

(3)   Lord, who throughout these forty days,
> For us didst fast and pray,
> Teach us with thee to mourn our sins,
> And close by thee to stay.
>
> As thou with Satan didst contend,
> And didst the vict'ry win,
> O give us strength in thee to fight,
> In thee to conquer sin.
> (Claudia Hernaman)

(4)   *To the familiar tune; the verses are from Psalm 26.*
> Just a closer walk with thee,
> Precious savior, still my plea;
> Daily walking close to thee,
> Let it be, dear Lord, let it be.
>
> Thou wilt never see me run
> With the false and wicked one;
> Wash my hands and cleanse my tongue!
> Let it be, dear Lord, let it be!
> (Paraphrase by John Ylvisaker)

(5) Praise to the Holiest in the height,
   And in the depth be praise;
   In all his words most wonderful,
   Most sure in all his ways!

O loving wisdom of our God!
   When all was sin and shame,
   A second Adam to the fight
   And to the rescue came.

O wisest love! that flesh and blood,
   Which did in Adam fail,
   Should strive afresh against the foe,
   Should strive, and should prevail.

(John Henry Newman)

Psalm 57:2–4, 7–9, 11

Have pity on me, O God; have pity on me,
   for in you I take refuge.
In the shadow of your wings I take refuge,
   till harm pass by.
I call to God the Most High,
   to God, my benefactor.
May he send from heaven and save me;
      may he make those a reproach who trample upon me;
      may God send his kindness and his faithfulness.
They have prepared a net for my feet;
      they have bowed me down;
They have dug a pit before me,
      but they fall into it.
My heart is steadfast, O God; my heart is steadfast;
      I will sing and chant praise.
Awake, O my soul; awake, lyre and harp!
      I will wake the dawn.
For your kindness towers to the heavens,
      and your faithfulness to the skies.

Scripture

*If the scripture is to be read with morning prayer, the reference will be
found in "Scripture Readings for Lenten Weekdays" in this chapter. All
are seated for the scripture and the silence.*

Silence

Prayer

Leader: Come back to me, says the Lord.
   All: Come back to me with all your heart.
Leader: Let us pray.
      Lord, hear the prayer of those who seek you,
      and let us rejoice in you.
      You are ever near to those who are of troubled heart;
      so listen to us
      and turn our whole lives to your peace
      which surpasses all our understanding.
This conclusion may be sung or spoken as all bow deeply:
Leader: Draw near, O Lord our God, graciously hear us,
   All: Guilty of sinning before you.
All make the sign of the cross in silence.

Alternate Psalms

Psalm 43:1–4

      Do me justice, O God, and fight my fight against a faithless
         people;
         from the deceitful and impious man rescue me.
      For you, O God, are my strength.
         Why do you keep me so far away?
      Why must I go about in mourning,
         with the enemy oppressing me?
      Send forth your light and your fidelity;
         they shall lead me on
      And bring me to your holy mountain,
         to your dwelling place.
      Then will I go in to the altar of God,
         the God of my gladness and joy;

Then will I give you thanks upon the harp,
O God, my God.

Psalm 130:1–7

Out of the depths I cry to you, O Lord;
Lord, hear my voice!
Let your ears be attentive
to my voice in supplication:
If you, O Lord, mark iniquities,
Lord, who can stand?
But with you is forgiveness,
that you may be revered.
I trust in the Lord;
my soul trusts in his word.
My soul waits for the Lord
more than sentinels wait for the dawn.
More than sentinels wait for the dawn,
let Israel wait for the Lord,
For with the Lord is kindness
and with him is plenteous redemption.

Lenten Evening Prayer

The prayer can take place simply around the cross and the
scriptures, or at the dinner table. In the latter case, all would
kneel for the first part of the prayer, then have the meal. Afterwards, all sit for the scripture and silence and stand for the final
prayer. A candle is placed near the cross or on the table. The
leader selects one or more verses of one of the songs.

Call to Prayer

The candle is lighted and all make the sign of the cross:
One lighting the candle: Light of Christ.
All: Thanks be to God.

Song

(*1*) Were you there when they crucified my Lord?
Were you there when they crucified my Lord?

Oh!—Sometimes it causes me to tremble, tremble, tremble.
Were you there when they crucified my Lord?

Were you there when they nailed him to the tree? . . .

Were you there when they pierced him in the side? . . .

(2) Amazing grace! how sweet the sound,
That saved a wretch like me!
I once was lost, but now am found,
Was blind, but now I see.

'Twas grace that taught my heart to fear,
And grace my fears relieved;
How precious did that grace appear
The hour I first believed!

The Lord has promised good to me,
His word my hope secures;
He will my shield and portion be
As long as life endures.

Through many dangers, toils and snares,
I have already come;
'Tis grace hath brought me safe thus far,
And grace will lead me home.

(3) 'Tis the gift to be simple, 'tis the gift to be free,
'Tis the gift to come down where we ought to be,
And when we find ourselves in the place just right,
'Twill be in the valley of love and delight.
When true simplicity is gain'd,
To bow and to bend we shan't be ashamed,
To turn, turn will be our delight
Till by turning, turning we come round right.

Psalm 27:1–5
The Lord is my light and my salvation;
whom should I fear?
The Lord is my life's refuge;
of whom should I be afraid?

When evildoers come at me
    to devour my flesh,
My foes and my enemies
    themselves stumble and fall.
Though an army encamp against me,
    my heart will not fear;
Though war be waged upon me,
    even then will I trust.
One thing I ask of the Lord;
    this I seek:
To dwell in the house of the Lord
    all the days of my life,
That I may gaze on the loveliness of the Lord
    and contemplate his temple.
For he will hide me in his abode
    in the day of trouble;
He will conceal me in the shelter of his tent,
    he will set me high upon a rock.

Scripture
The scripture for each day is taken from "Scripture Readings for Lenten Weekdays" in this chapter. All sit for the scripture and for the silence and intercessions.

Silence

Prayers of Intercession
Leader: We have listened to your word, O God,
    as you speak to us of. . . .
    May this word be our strength for the journey of Lent
    as we walk with Jesus.
    We pray especially . . .
(Here various prayers of intercession and thanksgiving may be made.)
    May the prayers we have spoken and those we keep in
    out hearts come before you, O Lord.

The Lord's Prayer
All stand and join hands to recite the Lord's Prayer.

Blessing

Leader: May God, who gently calls us to turn to him with all our
     heart, bless us and keep us in peace.

All make the sign of the cross.

Alternate Psalm

Psalm 102:2–5, 7–8, 10, 25–29

O Lord, hear my prayer,
    and let my cry come to you.
Hide not your face from me
    in the day of my distress.
Incline your ear to me;
    in the day when I call, answer me speedily.
For my days vanish like smoke,
    and my bones burn like fire.
Withered and dried up like grass is my heart;
    I forget to eat my bread.
I am like a desert owl;
    I have become like an owl among the ruins.
I am sleepless, and I moan;
    I am like a sparrow alone on the housetop.
For I eat ashes like bread
    and mingle my drink with tears.
I say: O my God,
Take me not hence in the midst of my days;
    through all generations your years endure.
Of old you established the earth,
    and the heavens are the work of your hands.
They shall perish, but you remain
    though all of them grow old like a garment.
Like clothing you change them, and they are changed,
    but you are the same, and your years have no end.
The children of your servants shall abide,
    and their posterity shall continue in your presence.

Scripture Readings for Lenten Weekdays

The readings from scripture for each weekday of Lent are given below. Readings for the Sundays of Lent will be found in Appendix I.

Ash Wednesday	Jl 2:12–18	Mt 6:1–6, 16–18
Thursday	Dt 30:15–20	Lk 9:22–25
Friday	Is 58:1–9	Mt 9:14–15
Saturday	Is 58:9–14	Lk 3:27–32
First Week		
Monday	Lv 19:1–2, 11–18	Mt 25:31–46
Tuesday	Is 55:10–11	Mt 6:7–15
Wednesday	Jon 3:1–10	Lk 11:29–32
Thursday	Est 12:14–16, 23–25	Mt 7:7–12
Friday	Ez 18:21–28	Mt 5:20–26
Saturday	Dt 26:16–19	Mt 5:43–48
Second Week		
Monday	Dn 9:4–10	Lk 6:36–38
Tuesday	Is 1:10, 16–20	Mt 23:1–12
Wednesday	Jer 18:18–20	Mt 20:17–28
Thursday	Jer 17:5–10	Lk 16:19–31
Friday	Gn 37:3–4, 12–13, 17–28	Mt 21:33–43, 45–46
Saturday	Mi 7:14–15, 18–20	Lk 15:1–3, 11–32
Third Week		
Monday	2 Kgs 5:1–15	Lk 4:24–30
Tuesday	Dn 3:25, 34–43	Mt 18:21–35
Wednesday	Dt 4:1, 5–9	Mt 5:17–19
Thursday	Jer 7:23–28	Lk 11:14–23
Friday	Hos 14:2–10	Mk 12:28–34
Saturday	Hos 6:1–6	Lk 18:9–14
Fourth Week		
Monday	Is 65:17–21	Jn 4:43–54
Tuesday	Ez 49:1–9, 12	Jn 5:1–3, 5–16
Wednesday	Is 49:8–15	Jn 5:17–30
Thursday	Ex 32:7–14	Jn 5:31–47
Friday	Wis 2:1, 12–22	Jn 7:1–2, 10, 25–30
Saturday	Jer 11:18–20	Jn 7:40–53

Fifth Week

Monday	Dn 13:1–62	Jn 8:1–11
Tuesday	Nm 21:4–9	Jn 8:21–30
Wednesday	Dn 3:14–20, 91–92, 95	Jn 8:31–42
Thursday	Gn 17:3–9	Jn 8:51–59
Friday	Jer 20:10–13	Jn 10:31–42
Saturday	Ez 37:21–28	Jn 11:45–57

Holy Week

Monday	Is 42:1–7	Jn 12:1–11
Tuesday	Is 49:1–6	Jn 13:21–33, 36–38
Wednesday	Is 50:4–9	Mt 26:14–25

Lenten Sundays

Because they are first of all Sundays, the Sundays of Lent are
not numbered with the forty days. Yet they do have much to do
with the shape of this season. The scriptures read on the Sundays, especially those of the A Cycle, are the principal scripture
stories of the season: the struggle of Jesus in the wilderness, the
transfiguration, the woman at the well, the man born blind, the
raising of Lazarus, and the story of Jesus' death.

The Sunday-welcoming Meal
*All as given in "The Sunday-welcoming Meal" in Chapter 2, but the
following blessing could be used over the cup of wine:*

> Blessed are you, Lord, God of all creation,
> Creator of the fruit of the vine.
>
> Blessed are you, Lord, God of all creation;
> you have taught us the way of holiness through your com-
> mandments
> and have granted us your favor
> and given us your holy Sabbath as an inheritance.
> This day is a memorial of creation
> in a season which marks the passover of all earth from
> death to life.
> This is a special day,
> a memorial of the breaking of the bonds of slavery and of
> sin and death

in a season which leads us to the freedom of God's children.

Blessed are you, O Lord; you make holy the Sabbath day.
As usual, the wine is then passed to everyone at the table.

Sunday Morning Prayer
The morning prayer for Lent, which is in this chapter, could be used, but with the special psalm below instead of the usual weekday psalm. After each verse spoken by the leader, all respond:
More precious than gold and sweeter than honey.

Leader: The Law of the Lord is perfect,
    refreshing the soul;
All: More precious than gold and sweeter than honey.
Leader: The decree of the Lord is trustworthy,
    giving wisdom to the simple.
All: More precious than gold and sweeter than honey.
Leader: The precepts of the Lord are right,
    rejoicing the heart.
All: More precious than gold and sweeter than honey.
Leader: The command of the Lord is clear,
    enlightening the eye.
All: More precious than gold and sweeter than honey.
Leader: The fear of the Lord is pure,
    enduring forever.
All: More precious than gold and sweeter than honey.
Leader: The ordinances of the Lord are true,
    all of them just.
All: More precious than gold and sweeter than honey.

Sunday Evening Prayer
All is taken from the "Leavetaking" rite in Chapter 2.

Lenten Meal Prayers
Table prayer during Lent takes on the mood of a season which draws us close to those who are hungry. Lent turns us toward those who were best able to listen to Jesus, wants to turn us *into* that sort of a people. Here are those who hungered honestly:

for food, for justice, for freedom, for knowledge, for closeness to God, for friends, for honesty, for decency. Our table prayer gives some voice to the solidarity we seek with all this hunger. This can be made quite real if the alms dish, mentioned in the introduction to Lent, is present at the table.

The prayer is a series of responses which will be quickly memorized.

Leader: I was hungry
    All: And you gave me food.
Leader: I was thirsty
    All: And you gave me drink.
Leader: I was a stranger
    All: And you welcomed me.
Leader: I was naked
    All: And you clothed me.
Leader: I was ill
    All: And you comforted me.
Leader: I was in jail
    All: And you came to visit me.
Leader: Lord Jesus Christ, may our Lenten fasting turn us
        toward all our brothers and sisters who are in need.
        Bless this table, our good food and ourselves,
        and send us on through Lent with good cheer.
        In the name of the Father and of the Son
        and of the Holy Spirit. Amen.

Stations of the Cross

This is a devotion that walks with Jesus. It centers on the last hours of Jesus' life, but does not forget the life and words and actions which caused the Roman occupiers of the nation to have Jesus executed. Marking these stations, we touch the anger and anguish that we feel before all suffering, our own and that of all creatures. We do not so much seek to understand it or to find a reason for it, but simply to find someone to stand with us, this Jesus who knew suffering so well.

The stations come when Christians, at Lent, realize that baptism is to die with Christ, to be plunged into his death, and this baptism lasts a lifetime. Jesus himself made baptism and death one reality when he spoke of the end of his own ministry: "I have a baptism to receive. What anguish I feel till it is over" (Luke 12:50). Affirming resurrection we are forever plunged into the sufferings of our world.

These stations can be prayed alone or together, in a church building, outside (where the idea of stations as a real pilgrimage originated), or at home. They juxtapose moments from Jesus' way of the cross with thoughts occasioned by some other human suffering. Many of these are from the scriptures which Jesus would have known well himself. Other prayers can be added, especially intercessions for those who suffer today and for our own selves who are pledged to stand with all who are in pain.

Opening Prayer

> May the cross of the Son of God, who is mightier than all
>   the hosts of Satan,
> and more glorious than all the angels of heaven,
> abide with us in our going out and our coming in.
> By day and by night, at morning and at evening,
> at all times and in all places, may it protect and defend us.
> From the assaults of evil spirits,
> from foes visible and invisible, from the snares of the devil,
> from all low passions that beguile the soul and body,
> may it guard, protect and deliver us. Amen.
>   *(From the Book of Common Prayer, Church of India)*

Before Each Station

This verse may be prayed before each station; it is customary to genuflect or kneel whenever it is said.

> We adore you, O Christ, and we bless you;
> for by your holy cross you have redeemed the world.

First Station: Pilate Condemns Jesus

> Pilate first had Jesus scourged; then he handed him over to
>   be crucified.
>   *(Based on Matthew 27:26)*

Then a new king, who knew nothing of Joseph, came to power in Egypt. He said to his subjects, "Look how numerous and powerful the Israelite people are growing, more so than we ourselves! Come, let us deal shrewdly with them to stop their increase. . . ." Accordingly, taskmasters were set over the Israelites to oppress them with forced labor. . . . The Egyptians, then, dreaded the Israelites and reduced them to cruel slavery, making life bitter for them with hard work in mortar and brick and all kinds of field work—the whole cruel fate of slaves.   (*Exodus 1:8–14*)

Between stations, it is traditional to sing a verse of the "Stabat Mater":
Careworn mother stood attending,
Witness to the bitter ending,
God, her Son, upon the tree.

Second Station: Jesus Carries the Cross
They led him off to crucifixion.
                              (*Matthew 27:31*)

It is cold and we have no blankets. The little children are freezing to death. My people, some of them have run away to the hills and have no blankets, no food; no one knows where they are—perhaps freezing to death. I want to have time to look for my children and see how many I can find. Maybe I shall find them among the dead. . . . I am tired; my heart is sick and sad.
                    (*From the words of Chief Joseph*
                    of the Nez Perces tribe at the time of surrender)

Though her soul was torn with aching,
Heart to heart she shared his breaking,
Piercing sword of agony!

Third Station: Jesus Falls
O wondrous change! Those hands, once so strong and active, have now been bound. Helpless and forlorn, you see the end of your deed. Yet with a sigh of relief you resign your cause to a stronger hand, and are content to do so. For

one brief moment you enjoyed the bliss of freedom, only to give it back to God, that he might perfect it in glory.
(From the prison writings of Dietrich Bonhoeffer)

Mother of the sole begotten
Grieved for him, forlorn, forgotten.
Gentle heart all sorrow knows.

Fourth Station: Jesus and Mary Meet

At midnight the Lord slew every first-born in the land of Egypt, from the first-born of Pharaoh on the throne to the first-born of the prisoner in the dungeon, as well as all the first-born of the animals. Pharaoh arose in the night, he and all his servants and all the Egyptians; and there was a loud wailing throughout Egypt, for there was not a house without its dead. *(Exodus 12:29–30)*

While she saw that great atoning,
From her sad heart softened moaning
To that glorious son arose.

Fifth Station: Simon of Cyrene Carries the Cross

On their way out they met a Cyrenian named Simon. This man they pressed into service to carry the cross.
(Matthew 27:32)

Later,
if you faced the death of bombs and bullets
you did not do it with a banner,
you did it with only a hat to
cover your heart.
You did not fondle the weakness inside you
though it was there.
Your courage was a small coal
that you kept swallowing.
If your buddy saved you
and died himself in so doing,
then his courage was not courage,
it was love; love as simple as shaving soap.
(From "Courage" by Anne Sexton)

Could a man for all his boldness
Watch unmoved in silent coldness
Christ's own mother suffer so?

Sixth Station: Veronica Wipes Jesus' Face

Blessed is the match that is consumed in kindling flame.
Blessed is the flame that burns in the secret fastness of the
heart.
Blessed is the heart with strength to stop its beating for
honor's sake.
Blessed is the match that is consumed in kindling flame.
(From the Hebrew of Hanna Senesch)

No one truly open hearted,
Seeing Mary broken hearted,
But would comfort her in woe.

Seventh Station: Jesus Falls

"Come, all you who pass by the way, look and see
Whether there is any suffering like my suffering,
     which has been dealt me
When the Lord afflicted me
     on the day of his blazing wrath.
"From on high he sent fire
     down into my very frame;
He spread a net for my feet,
     and overthrew me.
He left me desolate,
     in pain all the day.
The Lord has delivered me into their grip,
     I am unable to rise.
(Lamentations 1:12–13, 14c)

Everyone dealt Christ the scourging,
Nailed him fast at evil's urging;
Mary saw his blood run red.

Eighth Station: The Women Weep for Jesus

A great crowd of people followed him, including women
who beat their breasts and lamented over him. *(Luke 23:27)*

Was not Jesus an extremist for love: "Love your enemies, bless them that curse you, do good to them which despite- fully use you and persecute you." Was not Amos an ex- tremist for justice: "Let justice roll down like waters and righteousness like an ever-flowing stream." Was not Paul an extremist for the Christian gospel: "I bear in my body the marks of the Lord Jesus." Was not Martin Luther an extremist: "Here I stand; I cannot do otherwise, so help me God." And John Bunyan: "I will stay in jail to the end of my days before I make a butchery of my conscience." And Abraham Lincoln: "This nation cannot survive half slave and half free." And Thomas Jefferson: "We hold these truths to be self-evident, that all men are created equal . . ." So the question is not whether we will be extremists, but what kind of extremists we will be. Will we be ex- tremists for hate or for love? Will we be extremists for the preservation of injustice or for the extension of justice?

(Martin Luther King, Jr., in his letter from a Birmingham jail)

She beheld her dear beloved
Left by all, by darkness covered,
Till his spirit fell and fled.

Ninth Station: Jesus Falls

Pharaoh was already near when the Israelites looked up and saw that the Egyptians were on the march in pursuit of them. In great fright they cried out to the Lord. And they complained to Moses, "Were there no burial places in Egypt that you had to bring us out here to die in the desert? Why did you do this to us? Why did you bring us out of Egypt? Did we not tell you this in Egypt, when we said, 'Leave us alone. Let us serve the Egyptians'? Far better for us to be the slaves of the Egyptians than to die in the desert." But Moses answered the people, "Fear not! Stand your ground, and you will see the victory the Lord will win for you today." *(Exodus 14:10–13)*

May his flesh and five wounds bind me!
Holy Mother, ever find me
Near my master crucified.

Tenth Station: Jesus Is Stripped of His Garments

They divided his clothes among them by casting lots; then they sat down there and kept watch over him.

(Matthew 27:35–36)

What keeps you from giving now? Isn't the poor man there? Aren't your own warehouses full? Isn't the reward promised? The command is clear: the hungry man is dying now, the naked man is freezing now, the man in debt is beaten now—and you want to wait until tomorrow? "I'm not doing any harm," you say. "I just want to keep what I own, that's all." Your own! . . . If everyone took only what he needed and gave the rest to those in need, there would be no such thing as rich or poor. After all, didn't you come into life naked; and won't you return naked to the earth? *(Saint Basil)*

One with you I weep in sadness.
All lifelong be this my gladness:
Knowing Christ in every pain.

Eleventh Station: Jesus Is Nailed to the Cross

When they came to Skull Place, as it was called, they crucified him there and the criminals as well. *(Luke 23:33)*

Faithful cross, a tree so noble
    Never grew in grove or wood;
Never leaf or blossom flourished
    Fair as on thy branches glowed;
Sweet the wood and sweet the iron
    Bearing up so dear a load.

Ah! relax thy native rigour,
    Bend thy branches, lofty tree!
Melt, O wood, in tender mercy!
    Christ, the King of Glory, see!
Veiled in human sin and sorrow,
    Slain, from sin the world to free.

(Fortunatus)

By his cross I stand abiding.
On this wood my life confiding,
One with you to bear all strain.

Twelfth Station: Jesus Dies
Then Jesus, uttering a loud cry, breathed his last.
(Mark 15:37)

I am a man who knows affliction
    from the rod of his anger.
He has worn away my flesh and my skin,
    he has broken my bones.
A lurking bear he has been to me,
    a lion in ambush!
He deranged my ways, set me astray,
    left me desolate.
He has broken my teeth with gravel,
    pressed my face in the dust;
My soul is deprived of peace,
    I have forgotten what happiness is;
I tell myself my future is lost,
    all that I hoped for from the Lord.
(Lamentations 3:1, 4, 10–11, 16–18)

Friend of Christ, I share his giving,
Jesus dying in my living;
All his precious wounds I wear.

Thirteenth Station: Jesus Is Taken from the Cross
Joseph took him down and wrapped him in the
    linen. *(Mark 15:46)*

After great pain, a formal feeling comes—
The Nerves sit ceremonious, like Tombs—
The stiff Heart questions was it He, that bore,
And Yesterday, or Centuries before?

This is the Hour of Lead—
Remembered, if outlived,
As Freezing persons, recollect the Snow—
First—Chill—then Stupor—then the letting go—
(Emily Dickinson)

Christ, may Mary be the portal,
Gateway to reward immortal,
When my soul is borne above.

Fourteenth Station: The Burial of Jesus

Joseph laid the body in a tomb hewn out of rock, in which
no one had yet been buried.   (*Based on Luke 23:53*)

The hand of the Lord came upon me, and he led me out in
the spirit of the Lord and set me in the center of the plain,
which was now filled with bones. He made me walk among
them in every direction so that I saw how many they were
on the surface of the plain. How dry they were! He asked
me: Son of man, can these bones come to life? "Lord God,"
I answered, "you alone know that." Then he said to me:
Prophesy over these bones, and say to them: Dry bones,
hear the word of the Lord! Thus says the Lord God to these
bones: See! I will bring spirit into you, that you may come
to life. I will put sinews upon you, make flesh grow over
you, cover you with skin, and put spirit in you so that you
may come to life and know that I am the Lord.
(*Ezekiel 37:1–6*)

When to earth my body's given,
Grant my spirit light of heaven,
There with Mary thee to love.

Closing Prayer

We worship you, O Lord, we venerate your cross
and we praise your holy resurrection.
Through the wood of the cross you brought joy to the
world. Amen.

The Easter Triduum

These are the days that follow Lent and are the heart of the
whole year. They are the final hours of preparation, then the
baptism of new members into the community and the renewal
of baptism which Easter brings to all Christians. Thursday eve-

ning, Friday, Saturday, and Easter Sunday are the passing over
from death to life, from slavery to freedom, from sin to the
grace of God. The story, images, and songs of Jesus' death and
resurrection permeate these days.

Holy Thursday
At the beginning of any prayer today:
> I give you a new commandment:
> Love one another as I have loved you.

The scriptures for today are 1 Corinthians 11:23–26 and John 13:1–15. And this song could be used with any tune of the "Tantum Ergo":
> On the night of that last supper
> Seated with his chosen band,
> He, the paschal victim eating,
> First fulfills the Law's command;
> Then as food to all his brethren,
> Gives himself with his own hand.

(Thomas Aquinas)

Good Friday
Today and tomorrow, until the vigil liturgy, the great prayer of
individual and community is the fasting, the Easter fast of joyful anticipation.
At the beginning of any prayer today:
> We adore you, O Christ, and we bless you
> For by your holy cross you have redeemed the world.

The scriptures for today are Isaiah 52:13–53:12 and readings from the passion. And this song could be used, again with any tune of the "Tantum Ergo":
> Faithful cross, thou sign of triumph,
> Now for us the noblest tree,
> None in foliage, none in blossom,
> None in fruit thy peer may be;
> Symbol of the world's redemption,
> For the weight that hung on thee!

(Fortunatus)

Holy Saturday
This is a day of quiet and continued fasting. The day's prayer might be simply the verses from Psalm 16 which follow. The ancient stories of our scripture have traditionally been read today in keeping vigil for the Paschal Feast. The book of Jonah is especially important. Some of the following might also be read:

Genesis 1:1–2:3	Exodus 1:8–2:10
Genesis 2:4–3:24	Exodus 2:23–3:22
Genesis 7:1–8:22	Exodus 12:21–42
Genesis 22:1–18	Exodus 14:15–15:1
Genesis 28:10–22	Isaiah 54:5–14
Genesis 45:1–46:4	Ezekiel 37:1–14

Keep me, O God, for in you I take refuge;
    I say to the Lord, "My Lord are you.
    Apart from you I have no good."
I bless the Lord who counsels me;
    even in the night my heart exhorts me.
I set the Lord ever before me;
    with him at my right hand I shall not be disturbed.
Therefore my heart is glad and my soul rejoices,
    my body, too, abides in confidence;
Because you will not abandon my soul to the nether world,
        nor will you suffer your faithful one to undergo cor-
        ruption.
You will show me the path of life,
    fullness of jobs in your presence,
    the delights at your right hand forever.

Easter Day
Prayers and blessings for the conclusion of the Easter Triduum will be found in the next chapter.

Passover
The festival of Passover is bound up with our keeping of Lent and our celebration of Easter. To the early church, with its roots in Jewish life and faith, Passover was the context, the environment, in which they could speak of the death and resurrec-

tion of the Lord. Passover was a way to understand what had happened in Jesus. Without this festival, there could have been no vocabulary for Jesus or his followers to speak of the meaning of his death and ressurection.

Passover was in Jesus' time, as now, a Jewish springtime holiday celebrating the exodus—liberation, deliverance, salvation. It was that event that had deeply expressed the care of the Lord for this people and had given shape to their community life. It was not kept merely as an anniversary of independence, but as the affirmation of a present reality: it was not for our ancestors only, but for us, that the Lord does these things.

The roots of the spring holiday go even deeper than this. Before the story of the exodus came to be told at this time of year, there was a celebration of spring itself by peoples who knew and acknowledged their dependence on the return of the warmth and the rains, the new life in field and flock. The renewal of life itself is bound up in the springtime—the possibilities for life to grow and reproduce in the human community. That is the most basic liberation, and it was upon this kind of holiday that Passover was able to happen at all, that new dimensions of human freedom and human covenant could be celebrated.

The ritual celebration of all this took shape in two basic human activities: the sharing of a meal and the telling of a story. The words and the foods and drink brought together all the dimensions of the holiday. Over centuries there have been minor additions and changes, but much of the ritual remains as it has been for thousands of years, still simple and strong enough to express what life and liberation are about.

Christians today celebrate the Passover with its ritual meal not simply because it gives us contact with the ritual as Jesus kept it every year, nor because some of the evidence indicates that it was the Passover meal that was Jesus' last supper with his friends. Rather, this ritual expresses elements of our faith which have sometimes been neglected. It gives us a context to understand in a very immediate and almost physical way what the death and resurrection of Jesus mean. It is also a possible bond between Christianity and the parent faith, Judaism. Over centuries Passover has been the occasion for hatred and violence toward Jews; perhaps now it is to be the occasion for recognition of common roots.

The ritual of Passover is a home ritual. But it may be the occasion for several families to come together, or at least for a family to invite other individuals from the community to their Passover meal. The preparations are part of the festivity and can be shared among all who are to partake.

The date of Passover depends on the Jewish lunar calendar. Since the date of Easter is also based on the moon, the two festivals usually come within a few days of one another. The seder, a word which means the "order" of the ritual, is celebrated in the evening which begins a new day. Thus if the first day of Passover is April 10, the seder would be the evening of April 9. Some Christians have had the custom of celebrating Passover on Holy Thursday or some other day of Holy Week, but it would seem best that, when possible, it be kept on the proper day. The first day of Passover will be:

> 1980 April 1
> 1981 April 19
> 1982 April 8
> 1983 March 29
> 1984 April 17

The following pages present a rather simple seder service. For those who wish to follow the ritual with more detail, there are many editions of the Passover Haggadah (the name of the book which presents the whole ritual; the word *Haggadah* means "narrative").*

Song is an important part in the seder. Some may be able to use various pieces in English or Hebrew from the Jewish seder, but most will probably be satisfied to use various spirituals or folk songs which contain something of the longing and the

---

* An expecially fine edition, available in hardcover or paperback, is *A Passover Haggadah: The New Union Haggadah*, edited by Herbert Bronstein and published by the Central Conference of American Rabbis, 790 Madison Avenue, NYC 10021. Many of the texts on the following pages are taken, with permission, from that edition.

triumph and thanksgiving expressed in the service. Some songs are given following the ritual.

The seder is characterized not only by its wealth of expressions in songs, stories, poems, lights, food and drink, and games, but also by the freedom to introduce additional elements which make the whole celebration urgent for our own time. Thus, in words or in music, there could be an expression of how this liberation, begun in Egypt thousands of years ago, continues now in the world, in our nation, in our community, in ourselves.

Preparations

There are several special foods which are part of the ritual and often of the meal itself:

• *The wine.* Four cups of wine are taken within the ritual, two before the meal is served and two afterwards.
• *The matzah.* This is usually purchased. Three separate matzah are needed for the ritual; each is a large, unleavened, cracker-like piece.
• *Parsley or other green herb.* This brings the green of the coming springtime.
• *The bitter herb.* This may be some horseradish root, or some other strong radish or other herb or vegetable.
• *The haroset.* This is a salad made to resemble the mortar which the slaves used in Egypt. It is made from finely chopped apples, chopped nuts, cinnamon and wine.

Also on the table may be a roasted bone from a lamb, a sign of the ancient Passover sacrifice; an egg, that universal symbol of springtime and the triumph of life over death; a cup of salt water in which the parsley is dipped.

The table is set with its most festive appearance. This would include:

• *Candles,* which are lighted as part of the ritual itself.
• *A special seder plate,* which is placed near the leader, and contains the parsley, bitter herb, and haroset (a small quantity). The bone and the egg may also be on this plate.
• *The matzah,* placed near this seder plate if not on it, with each of the three pieces enclosed in the folds of a fine napkin.

• *The cup for Elijah.* This should be a very fine cup; it is filled with wine for the visit of the prophet.

Each participant needs a wine cup and plate and whatever else will be necessary for the meal. In addition to involving the whole family in the preparation of the foods and the table, special place cards can be made when guests are coming for the seder. When setting the table, there is sometimes one extra place set to symbolize those who are not yet free and so remind us that until they too can celebrate freedom, our own freedom is not fully realized.

The dinner itself can consist of any festive foods along with the wine and matzah and usually more of the haroset.

Other preparations include the housecleaning before such a celebration. In Jewish homes this is very much a part of the ritual since it centers on the search for and removal of all leavened bread and other foods containing yeast which are to be banished from the home during the eight days of Passover.

Another preparation involves the one who is to be the leader giving careful attention to the text so that everyone may be given some part in the rite: a question, a speech, a song, a musical piece, the filling of the wine glasses, the washing of hands, and so on. If possible, everyone should be able to practice these parts and to know when they come and what is involved. Parts to be spoken by all should be copied out on cards with the words to songs. With good preparation, the ritual can be a rich combination of the formal and the informal. A good structure for the rite will be the best preparation for the spontaneous moments of questions, laughter and discussion. An overview of the whole service would show the following elements:

- Sanctification of the day
- Lighting of the candles
- The first cup
- The parsley or green herb
- Breaking the middle matzah
- The four questions

- The narration of the story and the second cup
- Washing the hands
- Eating the matzah
- The bitter herb
- The meal
- The search for the matzah; dessert
- The thanksgiving including the third cup, the cup of Elijah, the psalms of praise, the fourth cup and conclusion

Note that parts marked "Leader" may be divided among others. Also, parts marked "group" may be spoken by all or by one.

The Passover Meal

Sanctification of the Day
When all are seated, the service begins. If appropriate, and especially if many are sharing in the seder for the first time, the leader may wish to speak first of some of the background to the festival as found above in the introduction to this section. In conclusion:

Leader: Now in the presence of loved ones and friends,
before us the emblems of festive rejoicing,
we gather for our sacred celebration.
Living our story that is told for all peoples,
whose shining conclusion is yet to unfold,
we gather to observe the Passover,
as it is written:

Group: You shall keep the Feast of Unleavened Bread, for on this very day I brought your hosts out of Egypt. You shall observe this day throughout the generations as a practice for all times.

Lighting the Candles
The one who lights the candles also speaks this blessing:
Blessed are you, Lord, God of all creation,
for you make our lives holy with your commandments
and command us to kindle festive holy light.

The First Cup: The Cup of Sanctification

All take up the cups filled with wine.

Leader: Blessed are you, Lord, God of all creation, Creator of the fruit of the vine. You have called us for service from among the people, and have hallowed our lives with commandments. In love you have given us festivals for rejoicing, seasons of celebration, this festival of Matzah, the time of our freedom, a commemoration of the exodus from Egypt.

Group: Blessed are you, Lord, God of all creation, for you have given us life, kept us safe, and brought us to this holy season.

All drink the first cup of wine.

The Parsley or Green Herb

All take some of the green herb and dip it in salt water, then say together:
> Blessed are you, Lord, God of all creation,
> Creator of the fruit of the earth.

Then all eat the green herb together.

The Breaking of the Matzah

The leader breaks the middle piece of matzah. One half will be hidden later so that the children may search for it at the end of the meal. The other half the leader holds up and says:

Leader: Among people everywhere, sharing of bread forms a bond of fellowship. For the sake of our redemption, we say together the ancient words which join us with our own people and with all who are in need, with the wrongly imprisoned and the beggar in the street. For our redemption is bound up with the deliverance from bondage of people everywhere.

Group: This is the bread of affliction, the poor bread,
which our ancestors ate in the land of Egypt.
Let all who are hungry come and eat.
Let all who are in want share the hope of Passover.
This year we are all still slaves.
Next year may all be free.

The Four Questions
Different children may then ask the questions.
• Why is this night different from all the other nights?
• On all other nights ,we eat bread of all kinds. Why tonight do we eat only matzah?
• On all other nights we eat all kinds of vegetables. Why tonight especially the bitter vegetables?
• On all other nights we eat in an ordinary way. Why all the ceremony tonight?

The Narration of the Story
The following is a very brief narration of the story. It can be done by the leader or by another or divided among several persons. It can be lengthened with greater detail on the exodus story and with other, more contemporary, examples of slavery and liberation.

We are slaves to Pharaoh in Egypt, and the Lord freed us from Egypt with a mighty hand. Had not the Holy One, praised be he, delivered our people from Egypt, then we, our children, and our children's children would still be enslaved. Therefore, even if all of us were wise, all of us people of understanding, all of us learned, it would still be our obligation to tell the story of the exodus from Egypt. For redemption is not yet complete.

My father was a wandering Aramean. He went down to Egypt with meager numbers and sojourned there, and there became a great and populous nation.

I took your father Abraham from across the river and I led him into the land of Canaan, and I increased his descendants; and I gave him Isaac and to Isaac I gave Jacob. When Jacob and his children went down into Egypt, Joseph was already in Egypt. Joseph had emerged with power over the land of Egypt. . . . There was famine in all lands, but in the land of Egypt, there was bread. And Pharaoh said to the Egyptians, "Go to Joseph; whatever he tells you, you shall do." And all the world came to Joseph in Egypt. After Joseph died and all his brothers and all that generation, a new king arose over Egypt who did not know Joseph. And he said to his people, "Look, the Israelite people are much too numerous for us. Let us, then, deal shrewdly with them, lest they increase, and in the event of war, join our enemies in fighting against us and gain ascendancy over the country."

So they set taskmasters over them with forced labor and they built garrison cities for Pharaoh: Pithom and Raamses. The Egyptians embittered their lives with harsh labor at mortar and brick and in all sorts of work in the fields. But the more they were oppressed, the more they increased and spread out, so that the Egyptians came to despise and dread the Israelites. So Pharaoh charged all his people, saying, "Every boy that is born shall be thrown in the Nile, but let every girl live." We cried unto the Lord, the God of our ancestors, and the Lord heeded our plight, our misery, and our oppression.

God heard our moaning, and God remembered his covenant with Abraham, Isaac and Jacob, and God looked upon the Israelites, and God said, "I will go through the land of Egypt on that night . . . and I will mete out justice against all the gods of Egypt. I the Lord."

(A song, such as "Go Down, Moses," may be sung here.)

And the Lord brought us out of Egypt by a mighty hand, by an outstretched arm and awesome power, and by signs and portents; not through a messenger, not through any intermediary or any supernatural being, but the Holy One, praised be he—he alone.

The time the Israelites remained in Egypt was four hundred and thirty years. At the end of the four hundred and thirtieth year, to the very day, all the hosts of the Lord departed from the land of Egypt. That same night is the Lord's watch-night for the children of Israel throughout their generations.

(All raise their wine glasses, which have been refilled.)

We praise the God who kept his faith with his people Israel. God's promise of redemption in ancient days sustains us now. For more than one enemy has risen against us to destroy us. In every generation, in every age, some rise up to plot our annihilation. But a divine power sustains and delivers us.

(All replace their wine glasses without drinking. At this point, additional stories or readings about the evil of human oppression and the demand for liberation could be added. And here all might sing "O Mary, Don't You Weep.")

When the Egyptian armies were drowning in the sea, the heavenly hosts broke out in songs of jubilation. God silenced them and said: "My creatures are perishing, and you sing praises?" So every triumph is diminished by the sufferings inflicted on the oppressor. So now let the wine within the cup of joy be lessened as we pour ten drops for the plagues upon Egypt. Every drop of wine we pour is hope and prayer that people will cast out the plagues that threaten everyone everywhere they are found, beginning in our own hearts. The making of war, the teaching of hate and violence, despoliation of the earth, perversion of justice and of government, fomenting of vice and crime, neglect of human needs, oppression of nations and peoples, corruption of culture, subjugation of science and learning and human discourse, the erosion of freedoms. We pour ten drops for the plagues upon Egypt.

(The leader may speak each plague; as all pour a bit of wine from cup to plate, they repeat the plague, shouting them out.)

Blood! Frogs! Lice! Wild beasts! Blight! Boils! Hail! Locusts! Darkness! Slaying of the first-born!

(Then all sing the Dayenu, a song of rejoicing. Dayenu means: That would have been enough! The group may wish to stand for this.)

Had he brought us out of Egypt, and not fed us in the
    desert,
Brought us out of Egypt we'd be satisfied.
(Refrain) Da-Dayenu, Da-Dayenu, Da-Dayenu, Dayenu,
    Dayenu.

Had he fed us with the manna, and not then ordained the
    Sabbath,
Fed us with the manna we'd be satisfied. *(refrain)*

Had he then ordained the Sabbath, and not brought us to
    Mount Sinai,
Then ordained the Sabbath we'd be satisfied. *(refrain)*

Had he brought us to Mount Sinai, and not given us the
  Torah,
Brought us to Mount Sinai we'd be satisfied. (*refrain*)

Had he given us the Torah, and not led us into Israel,
Given us the Torah we'd be satisfied. (*refrain*)

(*Then different members of the group may point to or hold up the various
objects on the table and explain them.*)

What is the meaning of this bone? In family groups, our
people ate the paschal lamb when the Temple was still standing. It was a reminder that God passed over the houses of our
ancestors in Egypt for they were marked with the blood of
the lamb.

What is the meaning of the matzah? Matzah recalls that the
dough prepared by our people had no time to rise before the
Exodus from Egypt. So we link ourselves to all the driven of
the earth as we fulfill the commandment: "For seven days
shall you eat matzah, that you may remember your departure
from Egypt as long as you live."

What is the meaning of this bitter herb? It is eaten because
the Egyptians made bitter the lives of our people.

In every generation, each person should feel as though it
was he or she who went forth from Egypt, as it is written:
"And you shall explain to your child on that day, it is because
of what the Lord did for me when I, *myself*, went forth from
Egypt."

Still we remember: "It was we who were slaves, . . . we who
were strangers." And therefore we recall these words as well:
"You shall not oppress a stranger, for you know the feelings
of the stranger, having yourselves been strangers in the land
of Egypt."

Not only our ancestors alone did the Holy One redeem but
us as well, along with them, as it is written: "And he freed *us*
from Egypt so as to take us and give us the land which he had
sworn to our fathers."

(Here again raise the wine cups and all say together:)
    Therefore, let us rejoice at the wonder of our deliverance
    from bondage to freedom, from agony to joy,
    from mourning to festivity, from darkness to light,
    from servitude to redemption.
    Before God, let us ever sing a new song:

    When Israel went forth from Egypt,
    Jacob's house from the alien nation,
    then Judah became his holy place,
    Israel his dominion. . . .

    Tremble, O earth, at the presence of the Lord,
    at the presence of the God of Jacob.
    He turns the rocks into pools,
    the flint into fountains.   *(Psalm 114)*

    Blessed are you, Lord, God of all creation,
    Creator of the fruit of the vine.
(All drink the second cup of wine.)

Washing the Hands
*With help from some of the children bringing water and towels, all wash
their hands in preparation for the meal. This blessing is said:*
    Blessed are you, Lord, God of all creation,
    for you have made us holy by your commandments
    and commanded us concerning the washing of the hands.

Eating the Matzah
The uppermost matzah is then broken and distributed to all. All pray:
    Blessed are you, Lord, God of all creation,
    for you bring forth bread from the earth.
Then all eat the matzah.

The Bitter Herb
*The pieces of bitter herb, dipped in the haroset, are then passed to all and
they pray:*
    Blessed are you, Lord, God of all creation,

for you have made us holy by your commandments
and commanded us to eat the bitter herb.
And all eat the bitter herb.

The Meal
The meal is then served, perhaps beginning with hard-boiled eggs as a
sign of new life. During the meal, someone hides the piece that was
broken from the middle matzah.

Search for the Matzah
When the children have finished eating, they may search for the hidden
matzah. The one who finds it gets a reward. This part of the matzah is
eaten as dessert.

The Thanksgiving
The following prayers and verses may be divided among all.
> Friends, let us say grace.
> The name of the Eternal be blessed from now unto eter-
> nity.
> Let us praise God of whose bounty we have partaken.
> By his goodness we live.
> On this Festival of Unleavened Bread, inspire us to good-
> ness.
> On this Day of Liberation, make us a blessing.
> On this Festival of Passover, preserve us in life.
> Make us worthy of a promise of a world that is yet to be.
>
> May he who blessed Abraham, Isaac, and Jacob
>   bless this house, this table, and all assembled here;
>   and so may all our loved ones share our blessing.
> The Lord will give strength unto his people.
>   The Lord will bless his people with peace.
> *(Then all take up the third cup of wine, the cup of blessing.)*
> Blessed are you, Lord, God of all creation,
> Creator of the fruit of the vine.
> *(All drink the third cup.)*
> The injustice of this world still brings to mind Elijah who in
> defense of justice challenged power. He reappears to help

the weak. May the All Merciful send us Elijah the Prophet
to comfort us with tidings of deliverance. Let us now open
the door for Elijah.

(A child opens the door to the outside. The cup of wine, filled for Elijah,
is sitting in a central place on the table.)

From beyond, Elijah's spirit enters in these walls
and tastes again with us the wine of endless promise.

(Then the Hallel Psalms, Psalm 115 to Psalm 118, may be read or
sung, or other songs of praise may be sung. Then the fourth cup is filled
and held up.)

Blessed are you, Lord, God of all creation,
Creator of the fruit of the vine.

(All then drink the fourth cup.)

Leader: Peace!
All: Peace!
Leader: Next year in Jerusalem!
All: Next year in Jerusalem!
Leader: Next year may all be free!
All: Next year may all be free!

In conclusion, an especially joyful song can be sung.

Passover Songs

(*1*)   When Israel was in Egypt land, Let my people go.
Oppressed so hard they could not stand, Let my people go.
Go down, Moses, way down in Egypt land;
Tell old Pharaoh: Let my people go!

No more shall they in bondage toil, Let my people go.
Let them come out with Egypt's spoil, Let my people go.
(*refrain*)

We need not always weep and mourn, Let my people go.
And wear these slavery chains forlorn, Let my people go.
(*refrain*)

O let us all from bondage flee, Let my people go.
And soon may all this world be free, Let my people go.
(*refrain*)

(2) O Mary, don't you weep, don't you mourn,
    O Mary, don't you weep, don't you mourn,
    Pharaoh's army got drownded! O Mary, don't you weep.
      River is deep and the river is wide;
      Milk and honey on the other side.
      Pharaoh's army got drownded! O Mary, don't you
        weep. (*repeat:* O Mary . . .)

      River Jordan is chilly and cold,
      Chills the body but not the soul.
      Pharaoh's army got drownded! O Mary, don't you
        weep. (*repeat:* O Mary . . .)

(3) We shall overcome, we shall overcome,
    We shall overcome some day!
    O—deep in my heart, I do believe
    We shall overcome some day.

    We are not afraid . . .
    We shall live in peace . . .
    We'll walk hand in hand . . .

(4) *To the tune of "Mine eyes have seen the glory . . ."*
    When the union's inspiration through the workers' blood
      shall run
    There can be no power greater anywhere beneath the sun.
    But what force on earth is weaker than the feeble strength
      of one?
    The union makes us strong!

      Solidarity forever! Solidarity forever!
      Solidarity forever! The union makes us strong!

    In our hands is placed a power greater than their hoarded
      gold,
    Greater than the might of armies magnified a thousand
      fold.
    We can bring to birth a new world from the ashes of the old
    For the union makes us strong! (*refrain*)

(5)   O Freedom! O Freedom! O Freedom over me!
      And before I'll be a slave, I'll be buried in my grave,
      And go home to my Lord and be free.

      No more slavery . . .
      No more hatred . . .

(6) Words of "Dayenu" are given within the service.

Chapter 6

✠✠✠

EASTERTIME

Introduction

The egg hidden under the bush in your front yard, the mythical rabbit who hid it there, the magic of this day's sunrise, the fire that is kindled in our churches to bring light and warmth, the water immersing and pouring over those who are entering the Christian church on this day, and that same water sprinkling over those who have just completed the discipline and renewal of Lent—all these revolve around what springtime means to us. It seems that only spring, in the midst of the city or in the countryside, is strong enough to call forth the celebration of our passovers: all the ways we once and always are moving from darkness to light, cold to warmth, slavery to freedom, death to life, emptiness to fertility (and fertility is where the egg and the rabbit and the easter candle plunged into the waters of the font come in).

Easter has its words that tell stories. It is, of course, a story about us. We drown, die with Christ, in the waters and live now by his peaceful breathing of the Holy Spirit. That's a passover. It happens to the individual, to the family, to the community. To color eggs, watch a sunrise, renew a baptism promise, give thanks once more at family table and church table and then eat and drink together—those are ways we sum up what these passovers mean. They are signs that say: the tombs are empty! The earth can live once more! The poor, the broken-hearted, the hungry, the oppressed, and all of these that is in each of us, can live!

The stories Easter has to tell and the wonder Easter is about take time to unfold. There is a calm and a peace about it all that will not be found in a day only. Easter is fifty days. It is the church's most ancient season with the festivals at either end existing first in the parent religion, Passover and Pentecost. Very early it was marked by prohibitions on kneeling and fasting.

This part of the book, then, has special blessings and prayers for Easter Day itself, meal prayers and daily prayers for these fifty days of Easter, a few notes on Sunday prayer, and special prayers to mark Ascension Day and Pentecost.

The prayer of this season springs from the church gathered at the font at the conclusion of the vigil liturgy of the Easter Triduum. The shivering, splashing, pouring, singing, dripping, warming, rubbing, oiling, clothing, hugging, blessing, breaking and sharing that happen there make Eastertime happen. The season itself is the deepest peace the church ever experiences. It is the powerful silence in which the seed sprouts, the bud swells, the tomb-become-womb is touched and understood. It is the unbelievably exciting tranquility of the walk to Emmaus, the stranger cooking breakfast by the lake, the meeting of Mary and Jesus in the garden, the farewell discourse in John's gospel. It is like the great wedding Jesus spoke of now and then, or that time in a wedding when "the moon is honey," as Dan Berrigan has said. The Song of Songs knew this feeling: "Come, then, my love, my lovely one, come. For see, winter is past, the rains are over and gone, the flowers appear on the earth, the season of glad songs is come, and the cooing of the turtledove is heard in our land."

Easter Day

The daily prayers for Eastertime, which will be found on the following pages, can be used, but with these verses on Easter Day only.

Rejoice, heavenly powers!
Sing, choirs of angels!
Exult, all creatures around God's throne!
Sound the trumpet of salvation!

Rejoice, O earth, in shining splendor,
radiant in the brightness of your King!
Christ has conquered! Glory fills you!
Darkness vanishes forever!

If there is a buried alleluia to be found, bring it back with
song: an "Alleluia" chant that is familiar and can be sung over
and over.

At breakfast, the Easter eggs may be blessed as all place their
hands on them:

> We praise you, O God, for these signs of life, our Easter
> eggs.
> We thank you for the bright, bursting forth of Christ our
> Lord.
> Let your blessing, Lord, come upon these eggs
> that they may be a health-giving food for the faithful
> who eat them in thanksgiving for the resurrection of
> Christ.
> Amen. Amen. Alleluia. Amen.

Easter water may be brought from the church, or the family
may bless water today to be used at prayer all through the
season. Clear water is placed in a fine bowl or other container
that can be kept throughout the season at the place of prayer.
This prayer is taken from the blessing of water at the Easter
Vigil.

> Father, at the very dawn of creation
>   your Spirit breathed on the waters,
>   making them the wellspring of all holiness.
> Through the waters of the Red Sea
>   you led Israel out of slavery.
> In the waters of the Jordan
>   your Son was baptized by John
>   and anointed with the Spirit.
> Your Son willed that water and blood
>   should flow from his side
>   as he hung upon the cross.

Fill this water with your blessing
   that it may refresh us, cleanse us,
   and bring us from death with Christ in our baptism
   to life with him forever.
Wherever this water is used
   may there be a spirit of goodness and of freedom from
     all harm.

Then everyone takes water and makes the sign of the cross, or someone may use a small evergreen branch, dipped in the water, to sprinkle everyone.

Eastertime Meal Prayers

This may be simply the passing of the Easter water for all to sign themselves with the cross. Then one holds up the water and says:

All to whom the saving waters come shall say: Alleluia!
And all sing an alleluia.

Or, if a candle is lighted to begin the prayer, the one lighting it could say:

The light of Christ, rising in glory. Alleluia!
And, again, all respond by singing an alleluia.

Or, the blessing could consist of a song or psalm from the various ones given below in morning and evening prayers for Eastertime.

Whatever blessing is used could conclude with this prayer:
God our Father, creator of all, this is our Easter joy.
May the risen Lord open our eyes
that we may know him in the breaking of bread.
Amen. Amen. Alleluia. Amen.

Eastertime Morning Prayer

The morning prayer of Eastertime might best take place in the light of the early rising sun. All stand, except to sit for the scripture and silence. At the beginning all take the Easter water and make the sign of the cross. The leader selects one of the songs for each day. An alternate psalm is given at the conclusion.

Call to Prayer
Leader: Christ is risen, Alleluia!
All: Christ is risen, Alleluia!

Song
(1) Jesus Christ is ris'n today, Alleluia!
Our triumphant holy day, Alleluia!
Who did once upon the cross, Alleluia!
Suffer to redeem our loss. Alleluia!

(2) Alleluia, Alleluia, Alleluia!
The strife is o'er, the battle done;
Now is the Victor's triumph won;
Now be the song of praise begun: Alleluia!

(3) *To the tune of "Ye Watchers and Ye Holy Ones":*
O Lord of all, with us abide
In this our joyful Eastertide;
Alleluia, Alleluia!
Your own redeemed forever shield
From every weapon death can wield.
Alleluia, Alleluia!
Alleluia, Alleluia, Alleluia!

(4) *To the tune of "Michael, Row Your Boat Ashore":*
Say, O wond'ring Mary, say, Alleluia!
What you saw along the way, Alleluia!

I beheld two angels bright, Alleluia!
Empty tomb and wrappings white, Alleluia!

I beheld the glory bright, Alleluia!
Of the rising Lord of light, Alleluia!

Psalm 114
When Israel came forth from Egypt,
the house of Jacob from a people of alien tongue,
Judah became his sanctuary,

Israel his domain.
The sea beheld and fled;
    Jordan turned back.
The mountains skipped like rams,
    the hills like the lambs of the flock.
Why is it, O sea, that you flee?
    O Jordan, that you turn back?
You mountains, that you skip like rams?
    You hills, like the lambs of the flock?
Before the face of the Lord, tremble, O earth,
    before the face of the God of Jacob,
Who turned the rock into pools of water,
    the flint into flowing springs.

Scripture
If the scripture is to be read at morning prayer, the reference will be found in "Scripture Readings for Eastertime Weekdays." All are seated for the reading and the silent time.

Silence

Prayer
All stand.
Leader: Once we were darkness, Alleluia!
    All: Now we are sunlight, Alleluia!
Leader: We seek and find in you the glory of the dawn. We seek and find you when the darkness of the night has fled. The sleep of faith has ever led through night to dawn. The sleep of faith will ever lead from death to life. Inspire us with your holy will in the beauty of the morn and send us forth to bless and purify all. Amen.

Doxology
In conclusion, all join hands and raise the hands high.
Leader: Praise God, all ye heav'nly host!
    All: Alleluia!
Leader: Father, Son, and Holy Ghost!
    All: Alleluia!

Alternate Psalm

Psalm 118:14–19, 24

My strength and my courage is the Lord,
    and he has been my savior.
The joyful shout of victory
    in the tents of the just:
"The right hand of the Lord has struck with power:
    the right hand of the Lord is exalted;
    the right hand of the Lord has struck with power."
I shall not die, but live,
    and declare the works of the Lord.
Though the Lord has indeed chastised me,
    yet he has not delivered me to death.
Open to me the gates of justice;
    I will enter them and give thanks to the Lord.
This is the day the Lord has made;
    let us be glad and rejoice in it.

Eastertime Evening Prayer

Whether at dinnertime or later, this prayer might take place
with the lighting of a candle, perhaps one that is new and special for the season. As for other Easter prayers, all stand. This is
the posture that speaks of resurrection and freedom. The
leader selects one of the songs for each day. An alternate psalm
is given at the conclusion.

Call to Prayer
The one lighting the candle says or sings:
    The light of Christ rising in glory!
And all respond with a sung or a shouted "Alleluia!"

Song
(*1*) Alleluia! Sing to Jesus! His the scepter, his the throne;
    Alleluia! His the triumph, his the victory alone:
    Hark! the songs of peaceful Sion thunder like a mighty
        flood,
    Jesus out of ev'ry nation hath redeemed us by his blood.
                                            (*William Dix*)

(2) *This is a verse from "The Strife is O'er, The Battle Done":*
Alleluia, Alleluia, Alleluia!
Lord, by the stripes that wounded thee
From death's dread sting thy servants free
That we may live and sing to thee: Alleluia!
Alleluia, Alleluia, Alleluia!

(3)   If I could I surely would
Stand on the rock where Moses stood.
Pharaoh's army got drownded! O Mary, don't you weep.
   O Mary, don't you weep, don't you mourn!
   O Mary, don't you weep, don't you mourn!
Pharaoh's army got drownded! O Mary, don't you
   weep.

Mary wore three links of chain,
Every link was freedom's name . . .

Moses stood on the Red Sea shore
Smotin' the water with a two-by-four . . .

The Lord told Moses what to do
To lead those Hebrew children through . . .

(4) *To its own tune, or to the tune of "Michael, Row Your Boat Ashore":*
Christ the Lord is ris'n today, Alleluia!
Sons of men and angels say, Alleluia!
Raise your joys and triumphs high, Alleluia!
Sing ye heav'ns and earth reply, Alleluia!

Lives again our glorious King; Alleluia!
Where, O death, is now thy sting? Alleluia!
Made like him, like him we rise, Alleluia!
Ours the cross, the grave, the skies. Alleluia!
(Charles Wesley)

(5) *To the tune of "Good King Wenceslaus":*
Through each wonder of fair days
 God himself expresses;
Beauty follows all his ways,
As the world he blesses:

So as he renews the earth,
Artist without rival,
In his grace of glad new birth
We must seek revival.

Praise the Maker, all you saints;
He with glory girt you,
He who skies and meadows paints
Fashioned all your virtue;
Praise him, prophets, heroes, kings,
Heralds of perfection;
Let us praise him for he brings
All to resurrection.

(Percy Dearmer)

The Song of Moses: Exodus 15:1-6, 16, 18
I will sing to the Lord, for he is gloriously triumphant;
    horse and chariot he has cast into the sea.
My strength and my courage is the Lord,
    and he has been my savior.
He is my God, I praise him;
    the God of my father, I extol him.
The Lord is a warrior,
    Lord is his name!
Pharaoh's chariots and army he hurled into the sea;
    the elite of his officers were submerged in the Red Sea.
The flood waters covered them,
    they sank into the depths like a stone.
Your right hand, O Lord, magnificent in power,
    your right hand, O Lord, has shattered the enemy.
Your people, O Lord, passed over,
    the people you had made your own passed over.
The Lord shall reign forever and ever.

Scripture
Daily readings from scripture will be found in "Scripture Readings for Eastertime Weekdays." All are seated for the reading and until the Lord's Prayer.

Silence

Prayers of Intercession

Leader: God of life, we thank you for the way you have shown us
in your servant, Jesus. In him we have our passover
from death to life as your children. We praise you in this
Eastertime for your loving care. This day we praise and
pray especially for . . .

(and here all may make prayers of praise and petition)
Now may we, your children, the church, fill our world
with this springtime love. We ask this in the name of
Jesus the Lord. Amen.

The Lord's Prayer

All stand and join hands to pray the Our Father.

Blessing

Leader: Stay with us, Lord, for it is getting dark.
May your blessing be always with us.
All: Amen! Alleluia!

Alternate Canticle

Revelation 19:1, 5–8

"Alleluia! Salvation, glory and might belong to our God,
for his judgments are true and just!
Praise our God, all you his servants,
the small and the great who revere him!
Alleluia! The Lord is king,
our God, the Almighty!
Let us rejoice and be glad,
and give him glory!
For this is the wedding day of the Lamb;
his bride has prepared herself for the wedding.
She has been given a dress to wear
made of finest linen, brilliant white.
Alleluia! Salvation, glory and might belong to our God,
for his judgments are true and just!"

Scripture Readings for Eastertime Weekdays

Readings for all Eastertime weekdays are given here. Sunday readings will be found in Appendix I.

First Week

Monday	Acts 2:14, 22–32	Mt 28:8–15
Tuesday	Acts 2:36–41	Jn 20:11–18
Wednesday	Acts 3:1–10	Lk 24:13–35
Thursday	Acts 3:11–26	Lk 24:35–48
Friday	Acts 4:1–12	Jn 21:1–14
Saturday	Acts 4:13–21	Mk 16:9–15

Second Week

Monday	Acts 4:23–31	Jn 3:1–8
Tuesday	Acts 4:32–37	Jn 3:7–15
Wednesday	Acts 5:17–26	Jn 3:16–21
Thursday	Acts 5:27–33	Jn 3:31–36
Friday	Acts 5:34–42	Jn 6:1–15
Saturday	Acts 6:1–7	Jn 6:16–21

Third Week

Monday	Acts 6:8–15	Jn 6:22–29
Tuesday	Acts 7:51—8:1	Jn 6:30–35
Wednesday	Acts 8:1–8	Jn 6:35–40
Thursday	Acts 8:26–40	Jn 6:44–51
Friday	Acts 9:1–20	Jn 6:52–59
Saturday	Acts 9:31–42	Jn 6:60–69

Fourth Week

Monday	Acts 11:1–18	Jn 10:1–10
Tuesday	Acts 11:19–26	Jn 10:22–30
Wednesday	Acts 12:24—13:5	Jn 12:44–50
Thursday	Acts 13:13–25	Jn 13:16–20
Friday	Acts 13:26–33	Jn 14:1–6
Saturday	Acts 13:44–52	Jn 14:7–14

Fifth Week

Monday	Acts 14:5–18	Jn 14:21–26
Tuesday	Acts 14:19–28	Jn 14:27–31
Wednesday	Acts 15:1–6	Jn 15:1–8
Thursday	Acts 15:7–21	Jn 15:9–11
Friday	Acts 15:22–31	Jn 15:12–17
Saturday	Acts 16:1–10	Jn 15:18–21

Sixth Week

Monday	Acts 16:11–15	Jn 15:26—16:4
Tuesday	Acts 16:22–34	Jn 16:5–11
Wednesday	Acts 17:15,22—18:1	Jn 16:12–15
Ascension	Acts 1:1–11	Mt 28:16–20
Friday	Acts 18:9–18	Jn 16:20–23
Saturday	Acts 19:23–28	Jn 16:23–28

Seventh Week

Monday	Acts 19:1–8	Jn 16:29–33
Tuesday	Acts 20:17–27	Jn 17:1–11
Wednesday	Acts 20:28–38	Jn 17:11–19
Thursday	Acts 22:30; 23:6–11	Jn 17:20–26
Friday	Acts 25:13–21	Jn 21:15–19
Saturday	Ex 19:3–8, 16–20	Jn 7:37–39

Eastertime Sundays

Sunday has long been for Christians a celebration of salvation in the resurrection of Christ. That is how this first day of the week, taking on much of the meaning of the Sabbath, became the original Christian feast day. During the Eastertime Sundays are most at home. The prayers for Sunday in Chapter 2 could be used as they are, or the following special prayer could be added Easter through Pentecost.

The Sunday-welcoming Meal

A sung alleluia could replace the usual hymn in welcoming the presence of Sabbath in the home. The prayer of blessing could be as follows:

Blessed are you, Lord, God of all creation,
Creator of the fruit of the vine.

Blessed are you, Lord, God of all creation;
you have taught us the way of holiness through your
    commandments
and have granted us your favor
and given us your holy Sabbath as an inheritance.
This is the day which the Lord has made,
the memorial of creation, ever new and beautiful.

This is the memorial of the passover,
the deliverance of our ancestors from slavery
and the raising of our Lord Jesus Christ.
Blessed are you, O Lord; you make holy the Sabbath day.

Ascension Day

The usual Eastertime prayers are used with the reading of Acts
1:1–11 and this song; it can be used with its own melody or that
of "Michael, Row Your Boat Ashore."

Hail the day that sees him rise, Alleluia!
To his throne above the skies; Alleluia!
Christ, awhile to mortals given, Alleluia!
Reascends his native heaven. Alleluia!

There for him high triumph waits; Alleluia!
Lift your heads, eternal gates; Alleluia!
He has conquered death and sin; Alleluia!
Take the King of glory in. Alleluia!   (*Charles Wesley*)

The following prayer could also be used today:
Father in heaven,
our minds were prepared for the coming of your kingdom
when you took Christ beyond our sight
so that we might seek him in his glory.
May we follow where he has led and find our hope in his
glory,
for he is Lord for ever. Amen.

Or use these verses from Psalm 68:33–36:
You kingdoms of the earth, sing to God,
chant praise to the Lord
who rides on the heights of the ancient heavens.
Behold, his voice resounds, the voice of power:
"Confess the power of God!"
Over Israel in his majesty;
his power is in the skies.

Awesome in his sanctuary is God, the God of Israel;
    he gives power and strength to his people.
Blessed be God.

Pentecost

The Eastertime concludes on the fiftieth day with the ancient
festival of Pentecost. At the time of Jesus, this was one of the
three great feasts of pilgrimage that brought Jews from all over
to Jerusalem to worship there. In the story as told in Acts 2, it
was on this festival that the Lord's Spirit filled his followers. The
notion of the Spirit of God was not new. For Jesus and his
ancestors it was rooted in the physical reality of the breath and
the wind: these were the signs of God's spirit and of that spirit in
persons and in the world. From very early times, Christians
found that this image of wind, breath, and spirit expressed
what they felt about God as present to them. Celebrate Pentecost by getting close to such things of the Spirit: blow, breathe,
inhale, exhale, hold your breath, run out of breath, chase the
wind, blow hard, inspire, expire, puff, gasp, wheeze, whistle, fly
kites, blow balloons, play wind instruments, make pin wheels,
receive the Holy Spirit.

    Here are some prayers that could be part of Pentecost:

Come, thou Holy Spirit, come!
And from thy celestial home
Shed a ray of light divine!
    Thou, of comforters the best;
    Thou the soul's most welcome guest;
    Sweet refreshment here below;
Come, thou Father of the poor!
Come, thou source of all our store!
Come, within our bosom shine.
    In our labor, rest most sweet;
    Grateful coolness in the heat;
    Solace in the midst of woe.
Heal our wounds, our strength renew;
On our dryness pour thy dew;
Wash the stains of guilt away.

Bend the stubborn heart and will;
Melt the frozen, warm the chill;
Guide the steps that go astray.
On the faithful, who adore
And confess thee, evermore
In thy sev'nfold gift descend.
Give them virtue's sure reward;
Give them thy salvation, Lord;
Give them joys that never end.

This prayer, by Black Elk, a Native American, could be a Pentecost prayer for Christians:

Hear me, four quarters of the world—a relative I am!
Give me the strength to walk the soft earth, a relative to all
that is!
Give me the eyes to see and the strength to understand,
that I may be like you.
With your power only can I face the winds.
Great Spirit, Great Spirit, my Grandfather,
all over the earth the faces of living things are all alike.
With tenderness have these come up out of the ground.
Look upon these faces of children without number
and with children in their arms,
that they may face the winds
and walk the good road to the day of quiet.
This is my prayer; hear me!
(*From* Black Elk Speaks, *edited by John Neihardt*)

Come Holy Ghost, Creator blest,
And in our hearts take up thy rest;
Come with thy grace and heav'nly aid
To fill the hearts which thou hast made,
To fill the hearts which thou hast made.

O Comforter, to thee we cry,
Thou heav'nly gift of God most high;
Thou Fount of Life, and Fire of Love,
And sweet anointing from above,
And sweet anointing from above.

Praise we the Lord, Father and Son,
And Holy Spirit with them one;
And may the Son on us bestow
All gifts that from the Spirit flow,
All gifts that from the Spirit flow.

Chapter 7

✤✤✤

CALENDAR

In the cycle of our weeks and years, and of family prayer as it marks these times, the calendar of Sundays, seasons, festivals and saints' days is an expression of our life within time, of our seeking for holiness within time, of our discovering the holy that is in our hours and days.

The calendar will always have elements that are universal for the church, that touch all Christians. But it must also be made particular, to the local church and even to the household. The calendars on these pages are therefore only beginnings. They date the feasts and Sundays of the next few years; they also go through the months, listing occasions of various kinds; some of these may be important to you, some will not. Your own important dates should be added.

The names given on the calendar below are drawn from the lists of holy men and women over the centuries. Most of these follow in the tradition of the recognized saints of the church. A number of others are included, historic figures of great importance to the work of good in our world. Some of these are quite recent. But all of these names are meant only as beginnings, only to suggest the kinds of persons that could find a place in our memory as we pray. Special thought might be given to adding the names of those who have enriched the spirit through the arts: through poetry, music, visual arts, drama, comedy, dance, and so on. In the same way, there are a number of martyrs of various sorts listed here, but many more who have helped to shape our freedom and our hope for freedom might be added.

The year given with a saint is, unless noted otherwise, the year of the saint's death, the birthday in heaven.

Some events have also been included on this calendar. Again, they are only to suggest some of the things that we ought to carry in our memory and sometimes remember in a very particular way. Each group using the book can gradually add both events and names to this calendar.

The individual or group leader of prayer can consult this calendar, as it is now and as it will grow with the addition of your own saints, in preparing the prayer for each day. Sometimes a special prayer has been provided (in which case the calendar will give a page reference), and sometimes it would simply be a matter of introducing the name into the prayer of the day.

Families can also write in their own festivals: anniversaries of weddings, births, baptisms, deaths, important moves, and whatever else you want to call to mind each year.

January

1	New Year's Day. Mary, Mother of God or Name Day See Chapter 4.	15	Birthday of Martin Luther King, Jr. See Chapter 8.
2	Basil and Gregory, fourth century.	16	
		17	Anthony, hermit and patron of all domestic animals, 356.
3		18	The Confession of St. Peter.
4	Elizabeth Ann Seton. See Chapter 8.	19	
5	John Newmann. See Chapter 8.	20	
		21	Agnes, martyred about 304.
6	The Epiphany of Our Lord. See Chapter 4.	22	
		23	
7		24	
8		25	The Conversion of St. Paul.
9		26	Timothy, Titus, and Silas.
10		27	Lydia, Doreds and Phoebe.
11		28	Thomas Aquinas, 1274.
12		29	
13	George Fox, 1691.	30	Gandhi, the Mahatma, assassinated in 1948.
14		31	

February

1	15 Susan B. Anthony's birthday,
2 Presentation of Jesus in the	1820.
Temple.	16
3 Ansgar, missionary to Denmark and Sweden, 865.	17
	18 Martin Luther, 1546.
4	19
5	20
6	21
7	22 George Washington's birthday, 1732.
8	
9	23
10	24 St. Matthias, Apostle.
11	25
12 Abraham Lincoln's birthday, 1809.	26
	27
13	28
14 Saint Valentine's Day. See Chapter 8.	(29)

March

1	17 Patrick, apostle of Ireland, about 464. See Chapter 8.
2 Charles Wesley, 1788, John Wesley, 1791.	
	18
3	19 Joseph, husband of Mary.
4	20 Time of the spring equinox. See Chapter 8.
5	
6	21
7 Perpetua and Felicity, martyred in Carthage about 202.	22 Jonathan Edwards, 1758.
	23
8	24
9	25 The Annunciation. See Chapter 8.
10 Harriet Tubman, 1913.	
11 Johnny Appleseed, preacher and planter, 1847.	26
	27
12	28
13	29
14	30
15	31
16	

April

1	All Fools' Day.	17	
2		18	
3		19	Warsaw Ghetto Uprising begins, 1943.
4			
5		20	
6	Albrecht Dürer 1528, Michelangelo 1567.	21	Anselm, Archbishop of Canterbury, 1109.
7		22	
8	Buddha's Birthday, 563 B.C.	23	Saint George. Shakespeare's birthday, 1564.
9	Dietrich Bonhoeffer executed, 1945.	24	
10		25	St. Mark the Evangelist.
11		26	
12		27	
13		28	
14		29	Catherine of Siena, 1380. See Chapter 8.
15			
16		30	

May

1	St. Philip and St. James, Apostles. Joseph the Worker. See Chapter 8.	17	
2	Athanasius, Bishop of Alexandria, 373.	18	Erik, King of Sweden, martyr, 1160.
3		19	Dunstan, Archbishop of Canterbury, 988.
4	Monica, Mother of Augustine, 387.	20	
5		21	
6		22	
7		23	
8		24	
9		25	
10		26	Augustine, First Archbishop of Canterbury, 605.
11		27	John Calvin, 1564.
12		28	
13		29	
14		30	Joan of Arc executed, 1431.
15	Isidore the Farmer. See Chapter 8.	31	The Visitation. Mary visits Elizabeth. See Chapter 8. Last Monday, Memorial Day. See Chapter 8.
16			

June

1 Justin, martyr at Rome, 165	17
2	18
3 Pope John XXIII, 1963.	19
4	20 Time of the summer solstice.
5 Boniface, missionary, martyr, 754.	See Chapter 8.
	21
6	22 Thomas More. See Chapter 8.
7 Seattle, Chief of the Duwamish Confederacy, 1866.	23
	24 Birthday of John the Baptist.
8	See Chapter 8.
9	25 Philipp Melanchthon, 1560.
10	26
11 St. Barnabas, Apostle.	27
12	28
13	29 St. Peter and St. Paul, apostles
14	and martyrs. See Chapter 8.
15	30
16	

July

1	16
2	17
3 Thomas, apostle.	18
4 U. S. Independence Day. See Chapter 8.	19
	20
5	21
6 Isaiah, prophet. Jan Hus, martyr, 1415.	22 Mary Magdalene, disciple. See Chapter 8.
7	23
8	24 Thomas à Kempis, 1471.
9	25 St. James, apostle.
10	26 Ann and Joachim, parents of
11 Benedict, monk, 540.	Mary. See Chapter 8.
12 Nathan Söderblom, archbishop of Uppsala, 1931.	27
	28 Johann Sebastian Bach, 1750.
13	29 Martha and Mary of Bethany.
14	See Chapter 8. St. Olaf, King
15 Saint Swithin's Day. Vladimir, first Christian ruler of Russia, 1015.	of Norway, martyr, 1030.
	30
	31

August

1	16
2	17
3	18
4 Anne Frank taken prisoner, 1944. See Chapter 8.	19
	20 Bernard, Abbot of Clairvaux, 1153.
5	
6 Innocents of Hiroshima, 1945. See Chapter 8. Feast of the Transfiguration.	21
	22
	23 Rose of Lima. Execution of Sacco and Vanzetti, 1927.
7	
8	24 St. Bartholomew, Apostle.
9 Innocents of Nagasaki, 1945.	25
10	26 Equal Rights Day. See Chapter 8.
11 Clare, companion of Francis, 1253.	
12	27
13 Florence Nightingale, nurse, 1910.	28 Augustine, Bishop of Hippo, 430.
14	29
	30
15 Mary, Mother of Our Lord, Feast of Assumption. See Chapter 8.	31 John Bunyan, teacher, 1688.

September

First Monday: Labor Day. See Chapter 8.	11
	12
1	13
2	14 Triumph of the Cross. Holy Cross Day. See Chapter 8.
3 Gregory the Great, 604.	
4 Moses, lawgiver and prophet. Albert Schweitzer, missionary, 1965.	15 Innocents of Birmingham, 1963.
	16
5 Crazy Horse assassinated, 1877.	17
	18 Dag Hammarskjold, peacemaker, 1961.
6	
7	19
8	20 Farm workers strike begins in Delano, 1965. Autumn equinox begins. See Chapter 8.
9 Peter Claver. See Chapter 8.	
10	

September *continued*

21 St. Matthew, apostle and evangelist.
22
23
24 Joseph, Nez Perce chief, 1904.
25

26
27 Vincent de Paul, 1660.
28 Wenceslaus, martyr, 935.
29 St. Michael and all angels. See Chapter 8.
30 Jerome, teacher, translator, 420.

October

1 Thersa of the Child Jesus.
2 Guardian Angels.
3 Woody Guthrie, 1967.
4 Francis of Assisi. See Chapter 8.
5 Tecumseh, 1813.
6 William Tyndale, translator, 1536.
7
8
9 Abraham and Sarah. See Chapter 8.
10
11
12 Columbus Day.
13
14
15 Teresa of Avila, teacher, 1582.

16
17
18 St. Luke, evangelist.
19
20
21
22
23 St. James of Jerusalem.
24 United Nations Day.
25
26
27
28 St. Simon and St. Jude, Apostles.
29
30
31 Halloween, the eve of All Saints. See Chapter 8. Reformation Day.

November

1 All Saints Day. See Chapter 8.
2 Remembrance of all the dead. See Chapter 8.
3 Martin de Porres.
4
5
6
7 Eleanor Roosevelt, 1962.

8 Dorothy Day's birthday, 1897.
9
10
11 Saint Martin's Day.
12
13 Frances Xavier Cabrini. See Chapter 8.
14

November continued

15
16
17
18
19
20
21
22
23
24

25 Isaac Watts, hymn writer, 1748.
26 Sojourner Truth, preacher of the gospel, of abolition, of equal rights, 1883.
27
28
29
30 St. Andrew, apostle.
Fourth Thursday, Thanksgiving Day. See Chapter 8.

December

1 Rosa Parks keeps her seat on a Montgomery bus, 1955.
2
3 Francis Xavier, missionary, 1552.
4
5
6 Nicholas Bishop of Myra, 342. See Chapter 3.
7 Ambrose, Bishop of Milan, 397.
8 Immaculate Conception of Mary. See Chapter 8.
9
10 Thomas Merton, 1968.
11
12 Our Lady of Guadalupe. See Chapter 8.
13 St. Lucy. See Chapter 3.
14
15 Bill of Rights ratified, 1791. Sitting Bull assassinated, 1890.

16 Beethoven's birthday, 1770.
17
18
19
20 The winter solstice begins. See Chapter 8.
21 St. Thomas, Apostle.
22
23
24 Christmas Eve.
25 Birthday of Jesus. See Chapter 4.
26 St. Stephen, deacon and martyr. See Chapter 4.
27 St. John, apostle. See Chapter 4.
28 Holy Innocents of Bethlehem. See Chapter 4.
29 Innocents of Wounded Knee. See Chapter 4.
30
31 New Year's Eve. See Chapter 4.

Chapter 8

✛✛✛

SAINTS' DAYS AND HOLIDAYS

Introduction

Our calendars have, besides their seasons, days of honoring and remembering. Sometimes this springs from an event in history: the signing of the Declaration of Independence, for example. Or such days recall the anniversary of a hero's birth or death: Lincoln's birthday, or the birthday of Martin Luther King, Jr., or the feast of Peter and Paul. Other days, whatever their origin, are shaped by certain customs: Valentine's, Thanksgiving, Mother's Day. Some of these sorts of days continue to have a vitality in our time, and some are fading. And some have taken on the artificial vitality of the commercial event.

Groups of people who share some common ground—a country, a faith, an occupation, a political outlook—need holidays as a way of sticking together, rallying to common ideals, remembering the past and keeping alive what was good and important. But such occasions depend on the very people who need them. *People* celebrate. *People* keep holidays. *People* remember. The special days have to be evoked, called forth, by what *we* do. They have their stories which are our story, but that story has to be told; we have to tell it to ourselves. Such days may also be marked with special prayer; suggestions for a few such days are given in this section. Many more days are mentioned on the calendar in the previous section.

Whenever possible, the prayer given here should be supplemented at some time during the day with at least some brief discussion of the life of the saint or the importance of the anniversary. The prayers themselves can be substituted for the usual prayer at the conclusion of the morning or the evening prayer.

Also in this section is a format for prayer during November. November is the time of harvest, of death or of death-like rest in much of nature. It has been the tradition to let this put us in mind of the saints, of all the dead, and of our own death. Though the Sundays and weekdays of November are a part of the church's "ordinary time," this month has something of a special character given to it by the festival of All Saints, the remembrance of all who have died, the Sunday feast of Christ the King that concludes each year a cycle of scripture reading, our own Thanksgiving Day. The month keeps death before our eyes.

Mary

The mother of Jesus is present in our prayers, in song, in the Hail Mary, in the invocation of the saints. She is honored also on special days of each year. In her we encounter the poor of Israel from whom came our own faith. In her we encounter a woman who witnesses that there can be preference given to "neither male nor female" in the faith of the church. In her we encounter one to be mother, to nurture us and to mirror for us how God loves us like a mother.

The principal feasts of Mary, and some of the scripture readings for those feasts are:

January 1	Mary, The Mother of God or Name Day. Luke 2:16–21.
March 25	The Annunciation. Luke 1:26–38
May 31	The Visitation. Luke 1:39–47
August 15	The Assumption. Luke 1:41–50
September 8	Birthday of Mary. Matthew 1:1–16
December 8	Immaculate Conception. Luke 1:26–38
December 12	Our Lady of Guadalupe. Luke 1:46–55

Morning or Evening Prayer on Feasts of Mary
The following format can be used for morning or evening prayer on Mary's days. The leader of prayer selects which song will be used.

Call to Prayer
After the sign of the cross:
Leader: Blessed are you among women.
   All: Blessed is the fruit of your womb.

Song
(*1*)   Sing of Mary, pure and lowly,
      Virgin-mother undefiled,
      Sing of God's own Son most holy,
      Who became her little child.
      Fairest child of fairest mother,
      God the Lord who came to earth,
      Word made flesh, our very brother,
      Takes our nature by his birth.

(*2*) *This verse of "Ye Watchers and Ye Holy Ones":*
      O higher than the cherubim,
      More glorious than the seraphim,
      Lead their praises, Alleluia!
      Thou bearer of th'eternal Word,
      Most gracious, magnify the Lord,
      Alleluia, Alleluia!
      Alleluia, Alleluia, Alleluia!

                              (*John Athelstan Riley*)

Canticle
Leader: Hail, Mary
   All: Full of grace; the Lord is with you.
Leader: My being proclaims the greatness of the Lord,
            my spirit finds joy in God my savior.
         For he has looked upon his servant in her lowliness;
            all ages to come shall call me blessed.

Hail, Mary
All: Full of grace; the Lord is with you.
Leader: God who is mighty has done great things for me,
　　　　holy is his name;
　　　His mercy is from age to age
　　　　on those who fear him.

Hail, Mary
All: Full of grace; the Lord is with you.
Leader: He has shown might with his arm;
　　　　he has confused the proud in their inmost
　　　　　thoughts.
　　　He has deposed the mighty from their thrones
　　　　and raised the lowly to high places.
　　　The hungry he has given every good thing,
　　　　while the rich he has sent empty away.

Hail, Mary
All: Full of grace; the Lord is with you.
Leader: He has upheld Israel his servant,
　　　　ever mindful of his mercy;
　　　Even as he promised our fathers,
　　　　promised Abraham and his descendants forever.
　　　　　　　　　　　　　　(Luke 1:46–55)

Hail Mary
All: Full of grace; the Lord is with you.

Scripture
One of the selections listed above, or one of the following: Luke 11:27–28; John 19:25–27.

Silence

Doxology
This verse from "Sing of Mary" may be sung or read.
　　Glory be to God the Father;
　　Glory be to God the Son;

Glory be to God the Spirit;
Glory be—our God is one!
From the heart of blessed Mary,
From all saints the song ascends,
And the church the strain reechoes
Unto earth's remotest ends.

Saints and Holidays

January 4, Elizabeth Ann Bayley Seton

Elizabeth Bayley was born in New York in 1774. After her husband's death she established schools and started a community of teaching sisters. She died in 1821.

Lord God,
you blessed Elizabeth Seton with gifts of grace
as wife and mother, educator and foundress,
so that she might spend her life in service to your people.
Through her example and prayers
may we learn to express our love for you
in love for our fellow men and women.
We ask this in the name of Jesus the Lord. Amen.

January 5, John Neumann

John Neumann was born in 1811 and came from Bohemia to the United States where he was ordained a priest and worked in the missions of the expanding nation. In 1852 he became bishop of Philadelphia. He died there in 1860.

Father,
you called John Neumann to labor for the gospel
among the people of the new world.
His ministry strengthened many others in the Christian
    faith:
through his prayers may faith grow strong in this land.
We ask this in the name of Jesus the Lord. Amen.

January 15, Birthday of Martin Luther King, Jr.
Martin Luther King, Jr. was 39 years old when he was assassinated in 1968. He had led the civil rights movement with nonviolent action and with the preaching of justice. Remembering him, we give thanks for the conscience he aroused and we keep alive the hopes he had.

> Lord, by the words and deeds of your servant Martin
> you freed people from the slaveries of body, of heart, or
>   mind.
> May his spirit breathe in every part of our land:
> "I have a dream that one day every valley shall be exalted,
> every hill and mountain shall be made low,
> the rough places will be made plain,
> and the crooked places will be made straight,
> and the glory of the Lord shall be revealed,
> and all flesh shall see it together."

February 14, Saint Valentine's Day
The feast of the martyred Bishop Valentine, legendary helper of people in love.

> Father, bless the love that brings people together
> and grows ever stronger in our hearts.
> May all the messages that carry the name of your holy
>   Bishop Valentine
> be sent in good joy and received in delight.
> We ask this in the name of Jesus the Lord. Amen.

March 17, Patrick
Born about 385, Patrick was sold as a slave in Ireland. He escaped, but came back to preach the gospel. He died in 461.

> May the road rise to meet you.
> May the wind be always at your back.
> And until we meet again, may the Lord keep you in the
>   palm of his hand.

When law can stop the blades of grass from growing as they
grow,
And when the leaves in summer time their color dare not
show,
Then I will change the color too I wear in my Caubeen.
But till that day, please God I'll stick to wearin' of the
green.

April 29, Catherine of Siena

Catherine was a scholar who brought peace between warring
cities and brought discipline and renewal to the church. She
lived from 1347 to 1380. This is one of her short prayers:

O Loving Madman!
Was it not enough for thee to become incarnate,
that thou must also die?

May 1, Joseph the Worker

May 1 has a long history, not only as a day of spring and of
exchanges between people in love, but more recently as an
international celebration of the dignity of labor. In part, this
sprang from the May 1, 1886 demand of the Federation of
Trades in New York City for an eight-hour working day. At
prayer today, use the song "Solidarity Forever." This can be
found at the end of the section "Passover" in Chapter 5.

May 15, Isidore the Farmer

Isidore farmed near Madrid in the twelfth century. His help is
asked for the fields and gardens. "The earth and all its fullness
is the Lord's."

Lord God,
all creation is yours, and you call us to serve you
by caring for the gifts that surround us.
May the example of Saint Isidore urge us
to share our food with the hungry
and to work for the salvation of all mankind.
We ask this in the name of Jesus the Lord. Amen.

Last Monday in May, Memorial Day
> Lord, make me an instrument of your peace;
> where there is hatred, let me sow love;
> where there is injury, pardon;
> where there is doubt, faith;
> where there is despair, hope;
> where there is darkness, light;
> and where there is sadness, joy.
> O divine Master, grant that I may not so much seek
> to be consoled as to console,
> to be understood as to understand,
> to be loved as to love.
> For it is in giving that we receive,
> it is in pardoning that we are pardoned,
> and it is in dying that we are born to eternal life.
>
> *(From a prayer of Saint Francis)*

June 22, Thomas More

Thomas More, a man of great learning and great humor, was executed July 6, 1535 because he would not accept the king as head of the church. "Assist me up, and in coming down I will shift for myself," he said as he went up the scaffold. And to his executioner: "Wait till I put aside my beard, for that never committed treason." Erasmus wrote of Thomas More: "There is nothing that occurs in human life from which he does not seek to extract more pleasure, although the matter may be serious in itself. . . . There is no one less guided by the opinions of the multitude, but on the other hand no one sticks more closely to common sense . . ." It was Robert Whittington who called More "a man for all seasons." In the play of that name, by Robert Bolt, More prays:

> I make my petition to Almighty God
> that he will keep me in this, my honest mind,
> to the last hour that I shall live.

June 24, Birthday of John the Baptist

At the summer solstice, when the days begin to grow shorter, just opposite Christmas, comes the birthday of John. Both birthdays have been festivals of light, as it begins to increase at Christmas and as it reaches its brightest and longest on John's birthday. This is from the song of Zechariah, John's father, as given in Luke's gospel.

> And you, O child, shall be called
> prophet of the Most high;
> For you shall go before the Lord
> to prepare straight paths for him,
> Giving his people a knowledge of salvation
> in freedom from their sins.
> All this is the work of the kindness of our God;
> he, the Dayspring, shall visit us in his mercy
> To shine on those who sit in darkness and in the shadow of
> death,
> to guide our feet into the way of peace.

June 29, Peter and Paul

Recall the stories that surround these two. Peter is called by Jesus from his life as a fisherman; he accompanies Jesus, along with James and John, at special times; he boldly answers Jesus' question about "Who do you say that I am?"; he says he is ready to go to execution with Jesus, then quickly denies he even knows who Jesus is; he outruns John to be at the tomb, and later, after early morning fishing and breakfast with Jesus, proclaims his love three times.

And Paul also. He gives us something of his own troubles in preaching the gospel: "I was stoned once, shipwrecked three times; I passed a day and a night on the sea. I traveled continually, endangered by floods, robbers, my own people, the Gentiles; imperiled in the city, in the desert, at sea, by false brothers; enduring labor, hardship, many sleepless nights; in hunger and thirst and frequent fastings; in cold and nakedness" (2 Corinthians 11:25–27).

> Father, we keep today the memory of the fisherman Peter
> and the tentmaker Paul, apostles and martyrs.
> Through their preaching, their courage, their humor
> and even their mistakes you brought the gospel to many.

Keep us close to their spirit,
strengthen all the churches with the eagerness of Peter
and the eloquence of Paul.
We ask this in the name of Jesus the Lord. Amen.

July 4, Independence Day

Father of the family of nations,
open our hearts to greater love of your Son.
Grant that the boundaries of nations
    will not set limits to our love,
and give us the courage to build a land
    that serves you in truth and justice.
We ask this in the name of Jesus the Lord. Amen.

We hold these truths to be self-evident: that all men are created equal, that they are endowed by their creator with certain unalienable rights, that among these are life, liberty, and the pursuit of happiness. That to secure these rights, governments are instituted among men, deriving their just powers from the consent of the governed; that whenever any form of government becomes destructive of these ends, it is the right of the people to alter or to abolish it, and to institute new government, laying its foundation on such principles and organizing its powers in such form, as to them shall seem most likely to effect their safety and happiness.

July 22, Mary Magdalene

Mary, disciple of our Lord: Pray for us.
Most dear to the heart of Jesus:
Constant woman:
Last at the cross of Jesus:
First at the tomb:
Apostle of apostles:
Advocate of sinners:
Spouse of the King of Glory:

July 26, Joachim and Ann
By legend, these were the names of Mary's parents. These verses from Psalm 128 would have been among their prayers.

> The Lord bless you from Zion:
>> may you see the prosperity of Jerusalem all the days of
>> your life;
> May you see your children's children.
>> Peace be upon Israel!

July 29, Martha and Mary
These were the friends of Jesus at Bethany, sisters of Lazarus.

> Lord, we remember as did Mary and Martha
> that our people have been strangers, have been away from
> home,
> have been even without a home.
> So may our doors be open to strangers and to friends,
> may we both give and find grace in hospitality.
> We ask this in Jesus' name, for he found rest in the home of
> Mary and Martha.

August 4, Anne Frank
On this day in 1944, after years of hiding in an attic, Anne Frank and her family and their companions were discovered, captured and sent to concentration camps. Anne was 15 years old. Only her father was alive nine months later when the war ended. Anne died at the camp at Bergen-Belsen in March, 1945. This day would be one of many on which to remember the Holocaust in which six million Jews died. The following, a meditation, is taken from the poetry of Nelly Sachs.

> O the chimneys
> On the ingeniously devised habitations of death
> When Israel's body drifted as smoke
> Through the air—

> O the chimneys!
> Freedomway for Jeremiah and Job's dust—
> Who devised you and laid stone upon stone
> The road for refugees of smoke?

August 6, Innocents of Hiroshima

On this day in 1945 the atomic bomb was used against this city in Japan. One hundred and fifteen thousand persons were killed and many times this number were made to suffer. Today, and on August 9 when Nagasaki was bombed, this prayer from a poem by Hermann Hagedorn:

> The bomb that fell on Hiroshima fell on America too . . .
> It burst. It shook the land.
> God, have mercy on our children.

August 26, Equal Rights Day

On this day in 1920 the right of women to vote was recognized. Luke 18:1–8 could be read as part of this day's prayer.

First Monday in September, Labor Day

> Almighty God, you have so linked our lives one with an-
>   other
> that all we do affects, for good or ill, all other lives:
> So guide us in the work we do, that we may do it not for self
>   alone,
> but for the common good;
> and, as we seek a proper return for our own labor,
> make us mindful of the rightful aspirations of other work-
>   ers,
> and arouse our concern for those who are out of work.
> We ask this in Jesus' name. Amen.
>
>   *(Book of Common Prayer)*

September 9, Peter Claver

Peter Claver ministered to the slaves who were being brought to the Americas. It is said: "His slavery to the slaves was the greatest reproach to those who considered themselves their masters." He came to Cartagena in Columbia in 1610 and worked without ceasing for the welfare of the slaves until his death in 1654.

> For the Lord shall rescue the poor man when he cries out,
>   and the afflicted when he has no one to help him.

He shall have pity for the lowly and the poor;
    the lives of the poor he shall save.
From fraud and violence he shall redeem them,
    and precious shall their blood be in his sight.

                             (Psalm 72:12–14)

September 14, Triumph of the Cross. Holy Cross Day.

Consolation of the poor: Save us, O holy cross.
Restraint of the powerful:
Destruction of the proud:
Refuge of sinners:
Hope of the hopeless:
Rest of the afflicted:
Safeguard of childhood:
Strength of adulthood:
Hope of the aged:
Wisdom of the foolish:
Liberty of slaves:

"Let the sign of the cross be continually made in the heart, the mouth, on the forehead, at table, at the bath, in bed, coming in and going out, in joy and sadness, sitting, standing, speaking, walking."

                             (John Chrysostom)

September 29, Michael and All Angels

Near the autumn equinox, strengthening us for the darker days ahead, stands Michael: "Who is like God?" In Daniel 10 and 12 he is the warrior angel on guard over the people; in Revelation 12 he leads the battle against the great dragon. So, when each year death and life struggle and death begins to gain the upper hand, this festival of Michael and all the angels affirms the faith we profess in a living God.

Be blessed, our stronghold, our Redeemer and King,
    Creator of holy beings;

praised be your name forever, our King, Creator of minis-
tering angels,
all of whom stand in the heights of the universe
and reverently proclaim in unison, aloud,
the words of the living God and everlasting King.
All of them are beloved, all of them are pure, all of them
are mighty;
they all perform with awe and reverence the will of their
Creator;
in serene spirit, with pure speech and sacred melody,
they all exclaim in unison and with reverence:
Holy, holy, holy is the Lord of hosts;
the whole earth is full of his glory.

October 4, Francis of Assisi

Francis lived from 1182 to 1226. He left a comfortable home to
become a beggar, a poet, a friend of people and animals, a
preacher of the gospel in word and deed. These lines are from
his song of all creatures. The translation is by Matthew Arnold.

O most high, almighty, good Lord God,
    to thee belong praise, glory, honor and all blessing!
Praised be my Lord God with all his creatures, and espe-
        cially our brother the sun,
    who brings us the day and who brings us the light;
    fair is he and shines with very great splendor;
    O Lord, he signifies to us Thee!
Praised be my Lord for our sister the moon, and for the
        stars,
    the which he has set clear and lovely in heaven.
Praised be my Lord for our brother the wind,
    and for air and cloud calms and all weather by which
        thou upholdest life
    in all creatures—
Praised be my Lord for our sister, the death of the body,
    from which no man escapeth.
Praise ye and bless the Lord,
    and give thanks unto him and serve him with great
        humility.

October 9, Abraham and Sarah

Many of the holy men and women who lived before Jesus are remembered on specific days in the Orthodox and Roman lists of saints. Abraham, the father of all believers, is mentioned in the martyrology on this day. Such days serve to remind that the communion of saints embraces a multitude of times and places.

> Abraham, father of many peoples,
>   kept his glory without stain:
> He observed the precepts of the Most High,
>   and entered into an agreement with him;
> In his own flesh he incised the ordinance,
>   and when tested he was found loyal.
> For this reason, God promised him with an oath
>   that in his descendants the nations would be blessed,
> That he would make him numerous as the grains of dust,
>   and exalt his posterity like the stars.
>   *(Sirach 44:19–21)*

> Lord, keep us, the children of Abraham and Sarah,
> faithful to your covenant.

For November 1, November 2, Christ the King, and Thanksgiving Day, see "November," below.

November 13, Frances Cabrini

Frances Cabrini was born in Italy in 1850 and came to the United States in 1889. From then until her death in 1917 she worked among immigrants, starting schools and hospitals.

> Yet with you I shall always be;
>   you have hold of my right hand;
> With your counsel you guide me,
>   and in the end you will receive me in glory.
> Whom else have I in heaven?
>   And when I am with you, the earth delights me not.
> Though my flesh and my heart waste away,
>   God is the rock of my heart and my portion forever.

> But for me, to be near God is my good;
> to make the Lord God my refuge.
>
> (*Psalm 73:23–26, 28*)

Equinox and Solstice Times

Although not included in the latest revision of the church's calendar, the tradition of marking these days with special prayer is quite ancient. In recent times they were known as the Ember Days and were kept with fasting, prayer, and often with the celebration of ordination. A family may wish to use these quarterly turning points as times to celebrate the sacrament of reconciliation (especially the winter and spring days which come during Advent and Lent), or to have special prayers of penance and forgiveness in the home. The prayers on page 190 may be used here. But special fasting and the giving of alms (of money or time or other gifts) would also be part of these days, as would some special attention to the day and night in their times of equality or greatest inequality.

November

Halloween is a festival that, in one form or another, is older than Christianity. From earliest times, when the cold and darkness of autumn began to take their hold on the earth and the air, folks began to think about death, about the dead. The church, when it announced the good news of Jesus Christ, found a new spirit for these autumn rites. The festivals of All Saints and All Souls and the whole keeping of November as a time of prayer for the dead came about this way.

The scriptures for the feast of All Saints and some of the November Sundays tell us that this is a time to consider how ". . . we are walking in the footsteps of those who've gone before, and we'll all be reunited . . ." That's as the old spiritual put it. It is a time when the dying all around in nature makes it easy to think about death, to get used to the idea of our own limitations, to think on all those friends, relatives, heroes and saints who have died.

As Christians, our vision of how death and life work together is quite different from that of the larger society. We look to Saint Francis who spoke of "Sister Death" and understood as well as anyone how life and death depend beautifully on one another.

Here is a format for morning or evening prayer during November. Following this are a number of other ideas for November, for Christ the King, and for Thanksgiving.

November Daily Prayer

A few fallen leaves could be used at the place of prayer to focus thoughts on life and death. The leader selects which song and which verses will be sung. Alternate psalms are given immediately following the prayer.

Call to Prayer

All make the sign of the cross.
Leader: We look for the resurrection of the dead
   All: And the life of the world to come.

Song

(1) O when the saints go marching in,
    O when the saints go marching in,
    Lord, I want to be in that number
    When the saints go marching in.
    (*Note: Make up new verses, naming your own family saints.*)

(2) For all the saints who from their labors rest,
    Who thee by faith before the world confessed
    Thy name, O Jesus, be forever blest,
    Alleluia, Alleluia!

    O blest communion, fellowship divine!
    We feebly struggle, they in glory shine;
    Yet all are one in thee for all are thine.
    Alleluia, Alleluia!

    From earth's wide bounds, from ocean's farthest coast,
    Through gates of pearl streams in the countless host,
    Singing to Father, Son and Holy Ghost:
    Alleluia, Alleluia!   (*William How*)

(3) Swing low, sweet chariot, coming for to carry me home.
Swing low, sweet chariot, coming for to carry me home.
   I looked over Jordan and what did I see,
   Coming for to carry me home;
   A band of angels coming after me,
   Coming for to carry me home.

(4) *This can be sung to the tune of "Faith of Our Fathers":*
   The saints of God, their wand'rings done,
   No more their weary course they run,
   No more they faint, no more they fall,
   No foes oppress, no fears appall.
   O happy saints! Forever blest,
   In that dear home, how sweet your rest!
                                    (*William Maclagan*)

Psalm 116:1–9

   I love the Lord because he has heard
      my voice in supplication,
   Because he has inclined his ear to me
      the day I called.
   The cords of death encompassed me;
      the snares of the nether world seized upon me;
      I fell into distress and sorrow,
   And I called upon the name of the Lord,
      "O Lord, save my life!"
   Gracious is the Lord and just;
      yes, our God is merciful.
   The Lord keeps the little ones;
      I was brought low, and he saved me.
   Return, O my soul, to your tranquillity,
      for the Lord has been good to you.
   For he has freed my soul from death,
      my eyes from tears, my feet from stumbling.
   I shall walk before the Lord
      in the lands of the living.

Scripture
Daily scripture readings for the weekdays of November will be found in Appendix II. Sunday readings are in Appendix I. All sit for the scripture and the silence.

Silence

Prayer
All stand and join hands.

Gracious Lord, in this season of fullness and completion,
we praise you for all living and all dying.
We thank you for that great circle in which we are united
with all who have gone before us.
Bring us all, good Lord, to the day when you will free our
eyes from tears,
our feet from stumbling,
when we shall walk before you in the land of the living.
We ask this in the name of Jesus the Lord. Amen.

Doxology
All bow deeply.
Leader: Jesus Christ is the firstborn of the dead.
Glory and praise be his forever!
All: Glory be to the Father and to the Son and to the Holy
Spirit
As it was in the beginning, is now and ever shall be,
world without end.

Alternate Psalm
Psalm 103:13–18, 22

As a father has compassion on his children,
so the Lord has compassion on those who fear him,
For he knows how we are formed;
he remembers that we are dust.
Man's days are like those of grass;
like a flower of the field he blooms;
The wind sweeps over him and he is gone,
and his place knows him no more.

But the kindness of the Lord is from eternity
to eternity toward those who fear him.
And his justice toward children's children
among those who keep his covenant
and remember to fulfill his precepts.

Keeping November in the Family

1. Make a litany of people who have died during the past year, people you wish to pray for during November. Remember family, neighbors, people who were famous, people who have no one else to remember them. Each night at supper, read some names from the litany and ask: "Lord, keep them all in your tender care and raise them up on the last day."
2. Make another litany, this one of saints. It may include those on the above litany, but also the past: your heroes, the saints of the church, great people of the Bible, people right off your family tree. Use the litany, with the usual "Pray for us" response, or this response: "Congratulations! The whole world awaits your return."
3. Do something about wills during November. Have one made, or updated. And talk about your funeral: the songs, casket, cremation, restoration of the body, the wake. Find out about memorial societies and donating the body to a medical school.
4. Make a pilgrimage to a cemetery. Cemeteries tell the story of our towns: where people came from, what languages they spoke, how long (or short) their lives were, how much they cared for beauty and/or simplicity by their tombstones. Take along paper and crayons or chalk and make rubbings of the stones.
5. Make the family tree during November, going as far back and as far out as possible. Note names, places, dates. Get help from relatives.

Christ the King

The last Sunday of Ordinary Time, the Sunday before Advent begins, is kept among Roman Catholics as the feast of Christ the King. It carries through the vision introduced on All Saints Day.

Almighty and merciful God,
you break the power of evil
and make all things new
in your Son Jesus Christ, the King of the universe.
May all in heaven and earth acclaim your glory
and never cease to praise you. Amen.

Thanksgiving Day

The meal prayer at dinner might be a litany of thanks to God
for all the ancestors and saints of the family, thus ending a
special November. Or it might be a scripture reading (such as
Colossians 3:12–17). Or a specially composed song: work with
the tune of "Row, row, row your boat . . ." and make up words
(e.g., "Thanks, Lord, thanks for all/Thanks for eyes and
mouth!/Thanks, thanks, thanks, thanks!/Thanks for north and
south!"). Or this prayer, from the liturgy for Thanksgiving Day:

Father all-powerful,
your gifts of love are countless
and your goodness infinite.
On Thanksgiving Day we come before you
with gratitude for your kindness:
open our hearts to concern for our fellow men and women,
so that we may share your gifts in loving service.
We ask this in the name of Jesus the Lord. Amen.

Chapter 9

✠✠✠

OCCASIONS

Introduction

The festivals and seasons, each with its own mood, come every year. The Sabbath visits every week, morning and evening every day. But there are other moments to be marked with prayer, many of them coming just now and again, sometimes expected and sometimes by surprise. They may be marked with excitement, or with sadness, or with hope, or with strange blendings of emotions. Sometimes the prayer of such moments is quite private, and sometimes there is a time for prayer together. The prayers that follow may be helpful in either case.

At the beginning, then, are prayers for birth and, at the end, prayers with the dying and for the dead. In between are the moments when life turns corners. Sometimes these involve the larger church community: baptism, confirmation and holy communion, marriage, reconciliation, the anointing of the sick. The prayers given here for such occasions are, with one exception, for the preparation or the thanksgiving that surround the church's ritual. That exception is the anointing of the sick which is normally celebrated at the home or the hospital. The prayers given here for anointing would be used with the celebration of the sacrament.

Other corner-turning moments are more the affair of the family: birth, leaving home and returning, moving from one home to another, blessings of gardens and fields, setting aside some of the family's money for sharing with others. Prayers for birthdays and wedding anniversaries are also given here.

The spirit of prayer in all these moments is thanksgiving. Thanksgiving is the very shape of our prayer. Our weekly liturgy is called eucharist, a word that means thanksgiving. The action we do there, the blessing and sharing of bread and wine, is a gathering up of what our lives have been and the strength for new living. The giving of thanks that happens over the gifts of bread and wine is the very shape of our Christian life. So when we come to the occasions of birth or of death, of parting or of reuniting, it is thanksgiving to the Lord that flows through our prayer. This is not simply a "Thanks, God, for . . ." with the enumeration of favors received. Rather, it is an attempt at putting in words the spirit that beats in our hearts and blows in our breathing every second of the day.

Birth

Prayer During Pregnancy
Be present, Lord, in this time for waiting,
this blessed time that makes for us a baby.
May this child be carried with love and tenderness,
with wonder for the way our lives are knit together,
with joy for the strange and wonderful ways of your world.

Unless the Lord build the house,
    they labor in vain who build it.
Unless the Lord guard the city,
    in vain does the guard keep vigil.
Behold, [children] are a gift from the Lord;
    the fruit of the womb is a reward.   (*Psalm 127:1, 3*)

At the Time of Birth
Lord, your love for us is like that of a mother
and you know the hard joy of giving birth.
Hold the hand of your servant now, keep her safe;
put your own spirit into her very breathing
and into the nostrils of the new baby whom we await with
    awe and hope.

In you, O Lord, I take refuge;
　　let me never be put to shame.
In your justice rescue me,
　　　incline your ear to me,
　　　make haste to deliver me.
Be my rock of refuge,
　　a stronghold to give me safety.
You are my rock and my fortress;
　　for your name's sake you will lead and guide me.
Into your hands I commend my spirit;
　　you will redeem me, O Lord, O faithful God.
(Psalm 31:1–4, 6)

Thanksgiving after Birth or Adoption

O God, we give you thanks for the blessing you have bestowed
upon this family in giving them a child.
Confirm their joy by a lively sense of your presence with them,
and give them calm strength and patient wisdom
as they seek to bring this child to love all that is true and noble,
just and pure, lovable and gracious, excellent and admirable,
following the example of our Lord and Savior, Jesus Christ.
(Book of Common Prayer)

Welcoming the Child into the Home

Good Lord, you have tenderly loved us,
given us this home and good friends.
Make us all to be a true home for this child
where (she, he) may learn trust in us and in you, Lord.
(May the brothers and sisters rejoice in their own growing up
as they help to care for this child.)

One thing I ask of the Lord;
    this I seek:
To dwell in the house of the Lord
    all the days of my life,
That I may gaze on the loveliness of the Lord
    and contemplate his temple.
For he will hide me in his abode
    in the day of trouble;
He will conceal me in the shelter of his tent,
    he will set me high upon a rock.

(Psalm 27:4–5)

Nurture of a Child

God, you are like a mother to us all,
nourishing all creatures with food and with blessing.
Strengthen my child with my milk and with the warmth of
    our nearness.

You send forth springs into the watercourses
    that wind among the mountains,
And give drink to every beast of the field,
    till the wild asses quench their thirst.
Beside them the birds of heaven dwell;
    from among the branches they send forth their song.
You raise grass for the cattle,
    and vegetation for men's use,
Producing bread from the earth,
    and wine to gladden men's hearts,
So that their faces gleam with oil,
    and bread fortifies the hearts of men.
They all look to you
    to give them food in due time.
When you give it to them, they gather it;
    when you open your hand, they are filled with good
    things.

(Psalm 104:10–12, 14–15, 27–28)

Baptism

This prayer is for parents on the eve of the baptism day:

> Praise to you, Lord Jesus, for the waters of baptism.
> In those waters your church is born,
> a people who know the struggles that lead from dying and
> rising.
> Bless this child whom we have named _____
> and count (her, him) in the number of your saints.
> May we promise with open eyes and willing hearts
> that by this baptism we mean to make a home where our
> child will find you,
> and so, in the delight of your Spirit, come to know the
> Father.
> All praise and all thanks to you, Lord Jesus, in your church
> forever.

For thanksgiving after the baptism, see the prayers of thanksgiving in Chapter 10.

Confirmation

With baptism, confirmation is an act of initiation into the church. Candidate and sponsors pray together in the time of preparation. The following section of this book, "Prayers and Devotions," contains many things that could be used during these times. The following prayer would also be appropriate.

> God our Father made us his children by the water of baptism:
> may he bless us and watch over us with his fatherly love.

> Jesus Christ the Son of God promised that the Spirit of
> truth
> would be with his church forever:
> may Jesus bless us with give us courage in professing the
> true faith.

The Holy Spirit came down upon the disciples
and set their hearts on fire with love:
may the Holy Spirit bless us, keep us strong in faith and
    love,
and bring us to the joy of God's kingdom.

(Adapted from the liturgy of confirmation)

First Communion

This prayer during the time of preparation for first communion
is a meal blessing. It would be used on occasions when there is
the leisure to treat the food and one another with reverence.
The sharing of food and fellowship at table is of vital importance in coming to know the mass as a meal of friendship and a
festive celebration.

Parent: Lift up your hearts!
  All: We lift them up to the Lord!
Parent: Let us give thanks to the Lord our God.
  All: It is right to give him thanks and praise.
Parent: Father, all creation depends on you;
        you open your hand and satisfy all our hunger.
        We give you thanks for your care in Jesus Christ our
            Lord.
        In him you call the church to your table
        where we bless and share bread and wine,
        the body and blood that makes us a holy communion.
        So at this table of ours we ask your presence
        and we join all earth and heaven in (singing, saying):
  All: *(A well-known version of the "Holy Holy" may be sung, or say
        together:)*
        Holy, holy, holy Lord, God of power and might!
        Heaven and earth are full of your glory!
        Hosanna in the highest!

For thanksgiving prayers in the days after first communion, see
the prayers of thanksgiving in Chapter 10.

Marriage

Blessing of the Engagement

In the presence of family and friends, perhaps after a festive meal together, a simple celebration of the engagement can take place. The man and woman stand facing each other and each promises to those present to prepare well for the marriage, then promises to the partner serious preparation and growth in love. Then the two join hands and parents and others can join in blessing them with hands outstretched over them or placed on their heads and shoulders:

> May the Father's love be in your promises.
> May the prayer of Jesus be in your lives.
> May the Spirit's joy blow all about you.

Prayer for Those Engaged

> We praise you, Lord, in times of waiting.
> May the days and hours not all be frenzy, but may I have good time
> to know my heart and to consider the promises we shall make.
> Thank you for _____, for (her, his) love;
> keep (her, him) in your gentle care these days.
> May you fill our hearts with awe before the covenant we are to make.
> Good Lord, be there always in sameness and in surprise,
> in good and bad times, now and always. Amen.

Blessing by a Parent

A blessing such as this could be given as part of the wedding or beforehand.

> May the Lord, who gave you to our care and made you a joy to our home,
> bless you and keep you.
> May the Lord, who turns the hearts of parents to their children

and the hearts of children to their parents,
smile on you and be kind to you.
May the Lord, who delights in the love of women and men,
turn toward you and give you peace.
May God bless you mightily today and always.

Thanksgiving
The prayers of thanksgiving in Chapter 10 could be used.

Reconciliation

These are prayers about sin, hurting and being hurt, forgiving,
forgetting. They express the tradition of our Jewish/Christian
faith that God forgives us like a parent, like a husband or a wife
whose love is greater than all, like a shepherd who celebrates the
finding of a lost sheep.

Use various parts of these prayers and scriptures in preparation for reconciliation, or as part of a family prayer when there
is need to celebrate reconciliation, or as a private prayer, perhaps at night. Prayers of sorrow for wronging others and
prayers asking forgiveness of the Lord and of others have traditionally been part of the prayer before sleep so that people do
not part for the night in anger or bitterness.

The family might plan to use some of these prayers rather
regularly, perhaps four times a year as was done with the
Ember Days. Together with fasting and extra almsgiving,
prayers of sorrow and reconciliation would then mark one or
more days near the end of Advent, near the end of Lent, at the
summer solstice and the autumn equinox. The latter two might
take the form of preparation for the feast of John the Baptist
(June 24) and of Michael and all angels (September 29).

Scripture Readings
The following scriptures are from those suggested for the rite
of reconciliation:
Genesis 4:1–15   Cain set on his brother and killed him.
Exodus 17:1–7   They tempted the Lord saying: Is the Lord
here or not?

Exodus 20:1–21   I am the Lord your God. You will have no other gods.

Deuteronomy 6:3–9   Love the Lord your God with your whole heart.

Deuteronomy 30:15–20   I set before you life and death.

2 Samuel 12:1–9, 13   Nathan said to David: The Lord has forgiven your sin.

Nehemiah 9:1–20   The people of Israel assembled for a fast and confessed their sins.

Isaiah 1:2–6, 15–18   I have nourished children and they have rebelled.

Isaiah 43:22–28   On account of me your iniquities are blotted out.

Jeremiah 2:1–13   My people have abandoned me, the fountain of living water.

Ezekiel 36:23–28   I shall sprinkle upon you clean water.

Hosea 2:16–25   I will make a covenant with them on that day.

Hosea 14:2–10   Israel, return to the Lord your God.

Micah 6:1–6   Do right and love mercy and walk humbly with your God.

Micah 7:2–7, 18–20   The Lord will turn back and have mercy on us.

Zechariah 1:1–6   Return to me, and I shall return to you.

Romans 5:6–11   We give glory to God through Jesus, our reconciliation.

2 Corinthians 5:17–21   God reconciled the world to himself through Christ.

Ephesians 2:1–10   When we were dead to sin, God brought us to life in Christ.

Ephesians 5:1–14   Once you were darkness; now you are light in the Lord.

James 1:22–27   Be doers of the word and not merely listeners.

James 2:14–26   What use to talk about believing and not show it in works?

1 John 1:5–2:2   If we confess our sins, he will forgive.

1 John 2:3–11   Whoever hates another remains in darkness.

1 John 4:16–21   God is love and the one who lives in love, lives in God.

Matthew 5:17–47 You have heard . . . but I say to you . . .

Matthew 9:1–8 Have confidence, my son, your sins are forgiven.

Matthew 9:9–13 I did not come to call the just, but sinners.

Matthew 25:31–46 What you have done to others you have done to me.

Luke 7:36–50 Her sins are forgiven because she loved much.

Luke 15:1–10 Heaven is filled with joy when one sinner turns back to God.

Luke 15:11–32 The prodigal son and the loving father.

John 8:1–11 Go and sin no more.

Prayers

(1) Have mercy on me, O God, in your goodness;
> in the greatness of your compassion wipe out my offense.

Thoroughly wash me from my guilt
> and of my sin cleanse me.

For I acknowledge my offense,
> and my sin is before me always:

"Against you only have I sinned,
> and done what is evil in your sight"—

That you may be justified in your sentence,
> vindicated when you condemn.

Indeed, in guilt was I born,
> and in sin my mother conceived me;

Behold, you are pleased with sincerity of heart,
> and in my inmost being you teach me wisdom.

A clean heart create for me, O God,
> and a steadfast spirit renew within me.

Cast me not out from your presence,
> and your holy spirit take not from me.

Give me back the joy of your salvation,
> and a willing spirit sustain in me.

(Psalm 51:3–8, 12–14)

(2) I confess to almighty God,
and to you, my brothers and sisters,
that I have sinned through my own fault
in my thoughts and in my words,
in what I have done,
and in what I have failed to do;
and I ask blessed Mary, ever virgin,
all the angels and saints,
and you, my brothers and sisters,
to pray for me to the Lord our God.

(3) Almighty and everlasting God, from whom and through whom and in whom all things are, from whose hand we, with all the world besides, every moment take our being: we appear before thee humbly to acknowledge that thou art the one true God, boundless in power, wisdom, goodness, the maker of all things made, the watchful witness and just judge of all things done.

Have mercy, O Lord, have mercy on us sinners. We repent of our sins, and wish them undone; they cannot be undone, but thou canst pardon them. We humply hope to be forgiven.

Help us for thy sake to love our neighbors, wishing them well, not ill; proposing to do them good, not evil; forgiving also all who have offended us, as we by thee hope to be forgiven.

This we ask through the merits of thy Son Jesus Christ our Lord, who liveth and reigneth with thee and the Holy Ghost one God, world without end.

(Prayer by Gerard Manley Hopkins)

(4) Lord Jesus Christ, you stretched out your hands on the cross and redeemed us by your blood: forgive me, a sinner, for none of my thoughts are hidden from you. Pardon I ask, pardon I hope for, pardon I trust to have. You are full of compassion and of mercy: spare me and forgive.

(Prayer of Saint Ambrose)

(5) For the sin which we have sinned against you under stress
     or through choice;
     For the sin which we have sinned against you openly or in
     secret;
     For the sin which we have sinned against you in stubborn-
     ness or in error;
     For the sin which we have sinned against you in the evil
     meditations of the heart;
     For the sin which we have sinned against you by word of
     mouth;
     For the sin which we have sinned against you by abuse of
     power;
     For the sin which we have sinned against you by the profa-
     nation of your name;
     For the sin which we have sinned against you by disrespect;
     For the sin which we have sinned against you by exploiting
     and dealing treacherously with our neighbor;
     For all these sins, O God of forgiveness, bear with us, par-
     don us, forgive us!

     (From the liturgy of Yom Kippur)

(6) Lord,
     hear the prayers of those who call on you,
     forgive the sins of those who confess to you,
     and in your merciful love give
     us your pardon and your peace.
     We ask this in the name of Jesus the Lord. Amen.

Examination of Conscience
     "Blessed are the poor in spirit,
     for theirs is the kingdom of heaven."
     Yet we are preoccupied with money and worldly goods
     and even try to increase them at the expense of justice.
     "Blessed are the gentle,
     for they shall inherit the earth."
     Yet we are ruthless with each other,
     for our world is full of discord and violence.

"Blessed are those who mourn,
for they shall be comforted."
Yet we are impatient under our own burdens
and unconcerned about the burdens of others.
"Blessed are those who hunger and thirst for justice,
for they shall be filled."
Yet we do not thirst for you, the fountain of all holiness,
and are slow to spread your influence
in our private lives or in society.
"Blessed are the merciful,
for they shall receive mercy."
Yet we are slow to forgive
and quick to condemn.
"Blessed are the clean of heart,
for they shall see God."
Yet we are prisoners of our senses and evil desires
and dare not raise our eyes to you.
"Blessed are the peacemakers,
for they shall be called children of God."
Yet we fail to make peace in our families,
in our country, and in the world.
"Blessed are those who are persecuted
for the sake of justice,
for the kingdom of heaven is theirs."
Yet we prefer to practice injustice
rather than suffer for the sake of right;
we discriminate against our neighbors
and oppress and persecute them.

("*Act of Repentance*" *from the ritual*)

Care of the Sick

The Rite of Anointing

In faith, the church community anoints and prays for those who
are sick. The illness may be of mind or body, or old age may also
be a reason for anointing. Children too may be anointed when
they are seriously ill. The sacrament should not be misused by

putting it off. The sacrament is not celebrated when the person has already died. All who take part in this liturgy should know that the rite is to be a symbol of the constant concern that all of us are to have for the sick.

Beforehand those who are to take part and, if possible, even the one or ones to be anointed, prepare. Scripture readings should be selected. The following is an outline of the liturgy.

Greeting

Scripture
There are very many scripture selections which speak of healing and of care for the sick. Any of these could be selected. Among them:

Isaiah 35:1–10   Strengthen the feeble hands.

Psalm 23   The Lord is my shepherd.

Psalm 27   Put your hope in the Lord.

Psalm 42   My soul longs for you, O Lord.

Acts 3:1–10   In the name of Jesus arise and walk.

Romans 8:18–27   We wait for the redemption of our bodies.

2 Corinthians 5:1, 6–10   (For the dying) We have an everlasting home.

James 5:13–16   The prayer made in faith will save the sick.

Revelation 21:1–7   (For the dying) There will be no more death or mourning.

Matthew 8:1–4   If you wish, you can cure me.

Matthew 8:5–17   Cures of the sick by Jesus.

Matthew 11:25–30   Come to me, all you who labor.

Luke 11:5–13   Ask and it will be given to you.

Litany
Then someone may lead this or a similar litany of prayer for the sick.

My brothers and sisters, with faith let us ask the Lord to hear our prayers for our (brother, sister).

(*Note: After each prayer there may be silence, or the response: "Lord, hear our prayer."*)

Lord, through this holy anointing, come and comfort (him, her) with your love and mercy.
Free (him, her) from all harm.
Relieve the suffering of all the sick.
Assist all those dedicated to the care of the sick.
Free our (brother, sister) from sin and all temptation.
Give life and health to our (brother, sister) on whom we lay our hands in your name.

Laying on of Hands

The one presiding then lays hands on the head of the sick person. Others present may do so also. This is done slowly and in silence.

Thanksgiving Prayer

This is said over the oil of anointing.

Leader: Praise to you, almighty God and Father.
You sent your son to live among us and bring us salvation.
Blessed be God.
(*Note: All repeat "Blessed be God" each time.*)
Praise to you, Lord Jesus Christ, the Father's only Son.
You humbled yourself to share in our humanity,
and you desired to cure all our illnesses.
Blessed be God.
Praise to you, God the Holy Spirit, the Consoler.
You heal our sickness with your mighty power.
Blessed be God.

Lord God,
with faith in you
our (brother, sister)
will be anointed with this holy oil.
Ease (his, her) sufferings
and strengthen (him, her) in (his, her) weakness.
We ask this through Christ our Lord. Amen.

Anointing
The sick person is anointed on the forehead and the hands.

> Through this holy anointing
> may the Lord in his love and mercy help you
> with the grace of the Holy Spirit. Amen.
> May the Lord who frees you from sin
> save you and raise you up. Amen.

Prayer after Anointing
The leader then prays for the one who has been anointed and asks all to join in praying the Our Father. Holy Communion may then be taken and the rite concludes with a blessing:

> May the Lord Jesus Christ be with you to protect you. Amen.
> May he go before you to guide you and stand behind you to give you strength. Amen.
> May he look upon you, to keep you and bless you. Amen.
> And may almighty God, the Father and the Son and the Holy Spirit, bless us all.
> Amen.

Prayers with the Sick
Many of the prayers, litanies and devotions in the next section of this book may be used. The following, from *The Book of Common Prayer,* are appropriate to various times.

For sleep:
> O heavenly Father, you give your children sleep for the refreshing of soul and body: Grant me this gift, I pray; keep me in that perfect peace which you have promised to those whose minds are fixed on you; and give me such a sense of your presence, that in the hours of silence I may enjoy the blessed assurance of your love; through Jesus Christ our savior. Amen.

In the morning:
> This is another day, O Lord. I know not what it will bring forth, but make me ready, Lord, for whatever it may be. If

I am to stand up, help me to stand bravely. If I am to sit still, help me to sit quietly. If I am to lie low, help me to do it patiently. And if I am to do nothing, let me do it gallantly. Make these words more than words, and give me the Spirit of Jesus. Amen.

In pain:

Lord Jesus Christ, by your patience in suffering you hallowed earthly pain and gave us the example of obedience to your Father's will: Be near me in my time of weakness and pain; sustain me by your grace, that my strength and courage may not fail; heal me, if it be your will; and help me always to believe that what happens to me here is of little account if you hold me in eternal life, my Lord and my God.

Blessing of a sick person:

May the almighty Lord, who created you out of nothing, give you his blessing.

May he heal your diseases, who is the only Lord and Redeemer.

And may he, our God, ever have you in his care, in whom is the fullness of your salvation.

Thanksgiving after Illness

See Prayers of Thanksgiving in Chapter 10.

Departing and Returning

This is a blessing when someone is leaving home for some length of time, or when the whole household is leaving on a trip or a vacation.

Along ways of peace may the almighty and merciful Lord lead (you, us).

May the angel Raphael accompany (you, us) on the journey.

So in peace, health and joy may (you, we) return to (your, our) own.

Show us your ways, O Lord, and lead us along your paths.

O God, you led your servant Abraham from his home
and guarded him in all his wanderings.
Guide these servants of yours now.
Be a refuge on the journey, shade in the heat,
shelter in the storm, rest in weariness,
protection in trouble and a strong staff in danger.
With your guidance may all reach the destination
and return safely home.

This prayer is for the return from a journey:
Blessed are you, Lord our God, for you lead us by separate
    ways
and you return us to one another.
In loving kindness you have given us a place to be at home.
We thank you for a safe journey.
Keep us in your care through all our pilgrimage
until we find our home with you.

Moving Away

The prayers above for departing and returning could be
adapted; the following is a prayer for a household moving from
one home to another. (See Chapter 4 for a house blessing on
Epiphany that could be adapted to bless a new home at any
time.)

God, our refuge always, our home is in you.
May this place where we have lived and found joys and
    sorrows
be filled with blessing for those who follow us here.
Protect us on our way, lead us to the strength of good
    friends,
help us to be a home to one another all our lives
till we come home to you.

Rogation Days

These have been days of special prayers for the crops, for the blessings of rain and good growing conditions. They are celebrated in the spring, and have often consisted of processions through the fields and the chanting of a litany. The following prayers could be used for blessing fields, gardens or just a window box on a good day in the spring. They are also appropriate for any Earth Day observance which celebrates the balance all creatures need to maintain for survival, goodness and beauty.

This may be recited or sung to the tune of "Amazing Grace," or "O God Our Help in Ages Past":

> Lord, in your name your people plead,
> And you have sworn to hear:
> Yours is the harvest, yours the seed,
> The fresh and fading year.
>
> Our hope, when autumn winds blew wild,
> We trusted you, O Lord;
> And still, now spring has on us smiled,
> We wait for your reward.
>
> The early and the latter rain,
> The summer sun and air,
> The green ear and the golden grain—
> All yours—are ours by prayer.   (*J. Keble*)

> Almighty God, Lord of heaven and earth:
> We humbly pray that your gracious providence may give
>   and preserve to our use the harvests of the land and of
>   the seas,
> and may prosper all who labor to gather them,
> that we, who are constantly receiving good things from
>   your hand,
> may always give you thanks;
> through Jesus Christ our Lord, who lives and reigns with
>   you and the Holy Spirit,
> one God, for ever and ever. Amen.
>   (*Book of Common Prayer*)

O merciful Creator, your hand is open wide
to satisfy the needs of every living creature:
Make us always thankful for your loving providence;
and grant that we, remembering the account that we must
  one day give,
may be faithful stewards of your good gifts;
through Jesus Christ our Lord,
who with you and the Holy Spirit lives and reigns,
one God, for ever and ever. Amen.

Sharing

This prayer may be used when the household is deciding on the use of some contribution of time or money to the church, to the poor, or to some institution, cause or group dedicated to worthy goals.

Father, yours is the earth and all the earth contains.
All that we have we have as gifts for this little while.
Help us now to share wisely the time and the wealth you
  give us,
always thanking you and rejoicing in the fullness of creation.
We ask this in the name of Jesus the Lord. Amen.

Birthdays

Almighty and everlasting God, maker of all creation,
listen to our prayer:
may this servant of yours who is celebrating (her, his)
  birthday
know many happy years, all of them pleasing to you.
We ask this in Jesus' name. Amen.

(Galasian Sacramentary)

May God, in whose presence our ancestors walked, bless you.

May God, who has been your shepherd from birth until now, keep you.

May God, who has saved us from all harm, give you peace.

(Based on Genesis 48:15–16)

On a birthday, or the anniversary of baptism, a person may wish to renew the promises made at baptism. This could be done as part of the blessing above, as the family prays on a birthday. The one renewing the promises simply responds to each of these questions.

Do you reject sin so as to live in the freedom of God's children?

Do you reject the glamor of evil and refuse to be mastered by sin?

Do you reject Satan, father of sin and prince of darkness?

Do you believe in God, the Father almighty, creator of heaven and earth?

Do you believe in Jesus Christ, his only Son, our Lord, who was born of the virgin Mary, was crucified, died, and was buried, rose from the dead, and is now seated at the right hand of the Father?

Do you believe in the Holy Spirit, the holy catholic church, the communion of saints, the forgiveness of sins, the resurrection of the body, and life everlasting?

Then all might pray the Lord's Prayer together.

Wedding Anniversary

Some of the prayers of thanksgiving in Chapter 10 would be appropriate. The following blessing, adapted from the wedding liturgy, could be prayed by the couple.

May God, the eternal Father, keep us in love with each other,

so that the peace of Christ may stay with us

and be always in our home. Amen.

May we find (blessing with our children)
consolation in our friends,
and peace in all people. Amen.
May we always witness to the love of God in this world
so that the afflicted and the poor will find us generous
    friends
and welcome us one day into the joys of heaven. Amen.
And may almighty God bless us, Father and Son and Holy
    Spirit. Amen.

Prayers with the Dying

The dying often want those around them to look at death with
them, not to pretend that everything will be all right, and not to
detract, out of our uneasiness, from the majesty of the last
hours. The church never denies death, but treats its approach
with humility and with confidence in God's promise. Many of
the prayers in the following section on "Prayers and Devotions"
could be used at the bedside of one who is dying. The following
are also appropriate. All such prayers are very much for the
sake of those who mourn.

Psalm 23

The Lord is my shepherd; I shall not want.
    In verdant pastures he gives me repose;
Beside restful waters he leads me;
    he refreshes my soul.
He guides me in right paths
    for his name's sake.
Even though I walk in the dark valley
    I fear no evil; for you are at my side
With your rod and your staff
    that give me courage.
You spread the table before me
    in the sight of my foes;
You anoint my head with oil;
    my cup overflows.
Only goodness and kindness follow me

all the days of my life;
And I shall dwell in the house of the Lord
    for years to come.

Psalm 31:2–3, 6, 10–11, 20, 25

In you, O Lord, I take refuge;
    let me never be put to shame.
In your justice rescue me,
    incline your ear to me,
    make haste to deliver me!
Into your hands I commend my spirit;
    you will redeem me, O Lord, O faithful God.
Have pity on me, O Lord, for I am in distress;
    with sorrow my eye is consumed; my soul also, and my
        body.
For my life is spent with grief
    and my years with sighing;
My strength has failed through affliction,
    and my bones are consumed.
How great is the goodness, O Lord,
    which you have in store for those who fear you,
And which, toward those who take refuge in you,
    you show in the sight of men.
Take courage and be stouthearted,
    all you who hope in the Lord.

Psalm 121

I lift up my eyes toward the mountains;
    whence shall help come to me?
My help is from the Lord,
    who made heaven and earth.
May he not suffer your foot to slip;
    may he slumber not who guards you:
Indeed he neither slumbers nor sleeps,
    the guardian of Israel.
The Lord is your guardian; the Lord is your shade;
    he is beside you at your right hand.

The sun shall not harm you by day,
    nor the moon by night.
The Lord will guard you from all evil;
    he will guard your life.
The Lord will guard your coming and your going,
    both now and forever.

Prayer

Be very near to us, Lord,
and hold our hands tightly in yours as your servant, gentle
    death, comes close.
For all that has been, we thank you,
and may we never be separated from you.
With all your saints now we await the resurrection and life
    everlasting. Amen.

Litany

All respond "Amen" to each short prayer.

Accept your servant, Lord, into the place of salvation for
    which (she, he) hopes.
Free your servant, Lord, from every pain and suffering.
Free your servant, Lord, as you freed Noah from the flood.
Free your servant, Lord, as you freed Abraham from his
    enemies.
Free your servant, Lord, as you freed Job from his suffer-
    ings.
Free your servant, Lord, as you freed Moses from the hand
    of Pharaoh.

At the Time of Death:

Various single invocations from the Litany of the Saints or other
litanies may be prayed over and over as death approaches. Or
one of the following:

Into your hands, O Lord, I commend my spirit.
Lord Jesus, receive my spirit.

In the name of God the almighty Father who created you,
in the name of Jesus Christ, Son of the living God, who
    suffered for you,
in the name of the Holy Spirit, who was poured out upon
    you,
go forth, faithful Christian.
May you live in peace this day,
may your home be with God in Zion.
Saints of God, come to (her, his) aid!
Come to meet (her, him), angels of the Lord!
May Christ, who called you, take you to himself;
May angels lead you to Abraham's side.
We commend our (sister, brother) N. to you, Lord.
Now that (she, he) has passed from this life,
may (she, he) live on in your presence.
In your mercy and love,
forgive whatever sins (she, he) may have committed
    through human weakness.
We ask this through Christ our Lord. Amen.

Free your servant, Lord,
as you freed Daniel from the den of lions.
Free your servant, Lord,
as you freed the three young men from the burning fire.
Free your servant, Lord,
as you freed Susanna from false witness.
Free your servant, Lord,
as you freed David from the attacks of Saul and Goliath.
Free your servant, Lord,
as you freed Peter and Paul from prison.
Free your servant, Lord,
through Jesus our Savior,
who suffered death for us
and gave us eternal life.

O Christ our God, you are the peace of angels and the
repose of all the elect:
mercifully bring your servant to rest in you.
And when (she, he) is raised from the sleep of death in the
Day of Judgment,
may (she, he) live joyfully with you in heavenly glory, world
without end. Amen.

Prayers after a Death

The following can be used as individual prayers at any time.
The whole service could be used by a family between death and
burial. This would be most fitting in the presence of the body,
but sometimes that is not possible.

Scripture

One or more of the following or other appropriate scriptures
may be read, with silence in between the readings.

Isaiah 25:6–9   The Lord will destroy death forever.

Lamentations 3:17–26   It is good to wait for the Lord to save.

Romans 6:3–9   Let us walk in newness of life.

Romans 8:31–39   Nothing can come between us and the love
of Christ.

1 Thessalonians 4:13–18   We shall stay with the Lord for ever.

Revelation 14:13   Happy are those who die in the Lord.

Revelation 21:1–7   There will be no more death.

Matthew 25:1–13   The bridegroom is coming; go and meet
him.

Luke 12:35–40   Be like those waiting for the arrival of their
master.

John 11:32–45   Lazarus, come out.

John 12:23–26   The grain of wheat falls into the ground and
dies.

Psalm

One of the psalms given above, or another appropriate psalm, is
chosen.

Reflection

A wake service should provide time for those who knew the dead person well to talk about the person's life. This could follow the prayer service, or could come as an informal time after the scripture and psalm and before the concluding prayers.

Prayers

Depending on the circumstances, appropriate prayers would be planned beforehand. These could be from among the favorite prayers of the deceased, or spontaneous prayers if the group is comfortable with this, or some of the prayers included in the following section "Prayers and Devotions." The following scripture selections could be read as meditations.

1. And to Adam God said: "Cursed be the ground because of you; in toil shall you eat of it all the days of your life; thorns and thistles shall it bring forth to you; and you shall eat the plants of the field. In the sweat of your brow you shall eat bread, till you return to the ground, since out of it you were taken; for dust you are and unto dust you shall return." *(Based on Genesis 3:17–19)*

2. There is an appointed time for everything, and a time for every affair under the heavens. A time to be born, and a time to die; a time to plant, and a time to uproot the plant. A time to kill, and a time to heal; a time to tear down, and a time to build. A time to weep, and a time to laugh; a time to mourn, and a time to dance. A time to scatter stones, and a time to gather them; a time to embrace, and a time to be far from embraces. *(Based on Ecclesiastes 3:1–5)*

3. We are short-lived and full of trouble. Like a flower that springs up and fades, swift as a shadow that does not abide. You know the number of our months; you have fixed the limit which we cannot pass. When we die, all vigor leaves us; when we die, then what are we?

(Based on Job 14:1, 2, 5, 10)

4. But as it is, Christ was risen from the dead, the first-fruits of those who have fallen asleep. As in Adam all die, so in Christ all will be made to live.

(Based on 1 Corinthians 15:20, 22)

5. And God will dwell with them. And they will be his people and God himself will be with them as their God. And God will wipe away every tear from their eyes. And death shall be no more; neither shall there be mourning, nor crying, nor pain any more, for the former things have passed away.

(Based on Revelation 21:3–4)

Prayers for the Mourners

Father,
God of all consolation,
in your unending love and mercy for us
you turn the darkness of death
into the dawn of new life.
Show compassion to your people in their sorrow.

Be our refuge and our strength
to lift us from the darkness of this grief
to the peace and light of your presence.

Your Son, our Lord Jesus Christ,
by dying for us, conquered death
and by rising again, restored life.

May we then go forward eagerly to meet him,
and after our life on earth
be reunited with our brothers and sisters
where every tear will be wiped away.
We ask this through Christ our Lord. Amen.

Grant, O Lord, to all who are bereaved the spirit of faith
   and courage,
that they may have strength to meet the days to come
with steadfastness and patience;
not sorrowing as those without hope,
but in thankful remembrance of your great goodness,

and in the joyful expectation of eternal life with those they
love.

And this we ask in the name of Jesus Christ our savior.
Amen.

Blessing

May our Lord Jesus Christ himself,
and may God our Father who loved us
and in his mercy gave us eternal consolation and hope,
console your hearts and strengthen them for every good
work and word.   (*2 Thessalonians 2:16–17*)

The prayer service or wake would conclude with this blessing.

Various Prayers for the Dead

For a young person:

Lord God, the days allotted to each of us
are in your fatherly care.
Though we are saddened
that our (sister, brother) N. was with us for so short a time,
we entrust (her, him) to you with confidence.
May (she, he) live, radiant and for ever young
in the happiness of your kingdom.
We ask this through Christ our Lord. Amen.

For one who suffered a long illness:

Lord God, in (her, his) suffering and long illness
our (sister, brother) N. served you faithfully
by imitating the patience of your Son, Jesus Christ.
May (she, he) also share in the reward of his glory
for ever and ever. Amen.

For one who died suddenly:

Lord, as we mourn the sudden death of our (sister,
brother) N.,
comfort us with the great power of your love
and strengthen us in our faith
that (she, he) is with you for ever.
We ask this through Christ our Lord. Amen.

For a young child:

Father, we entrust to you this child
whom you loved so much in this life.
Welcome (her, him) into paradise
where there will be no more sorrow,
no more weeping or pain,
but only peace and joy
with your Son and the Holy Spirit
for ever and ever. Amen.

For anyone who has died:

Almighty Father,
eternal God,
hear our prayers
for your (daughter, son) N.,
whom you have called from this life to yourself.
Grant (her, him) light, happiness, and peace.
Let (her, him) pass in safety through the gates of death,
and live for ever with all your saints
in the light you promised to Abraham
and to all his descendants in faith.
Guard (her, him) from all harm
and on that great day of resurrection and reward
raise (her, him) up with all your saints.
Pardon (her, his) sins
and give (her, him) eternal life in your kingdom.
We ask this through Christ our Lord. Amen.

For ourselves:

O God, whose days are without end and whose mercies
cannot be numbered:
Make us, we pray, deeply aware of the shortness and un-
certainty of human life;
and let your Holy Spirit lead us in holiness and righteousness all our days;
that, when we shall have served you in our generation,
we may be gathered to our ancestors, having the testimony
of a good conscience,
in the communion of the Church,
in the confidence of a certain faith,

in the comfort of a religious and holy hope,
in favor with you, our God, and in perfect charity with the
  world.
All this we ask through Jesus Christ our Lord. Amen.

Chapter 10

✛✛✛

PRAYERS AND DEVOTIONS

Litanies

The litany is a form of prayer that runs through most of the world's religions. It has the greatest simplicity, the repetition of a phrase that lets the one praying enter into a whole rhythm of physical and spiritual involvement. It is found in the Sunday eucharistic liturgy in one form in the prayers of intercession, in another in the "Lamb of God," and, on occasion, also in the "Kyrie." Below are three litanies, of which one is a psalm and another is from the Jewish prayerbook.

Litany of the Most Holy Name of Jesus

Jesus, son of the living God:
    have mercy on us.
Jesus, splendor of the Father:
Jesus, brightness of eternal light:
Jesus, king of glory:
Jesus, sun of justice:
Jesus, son of the virgin Mary:
Jesus, most amiable:
Jesus, most admirable:
Jesus, mighty God:
Jesus, father of the world to come:

Jesus, angel of the great counsel:
Jesus, most powerful:
Jesus, most patient:
Jesus, most obedient:
Jesus, meek and humble of heart:
Jesus, lover of chastity:
Jesus, lover of us:
Jesus, God of peace:
Jesus, author of life:
Jesus, model of virtues:

Jesus, zealous for souls:
Jesus, our God:
Jesus, our refuge:
Jesus, father of the poor:
Jesus, treasure of the faithful:
Jesus, good shepherd:
Jesus, true light:
Jesus, eternal wisdom:
Jesus, infinite goodness:

Jesus, our way and our life:
Jesus, joy of angels:
Jesus, king of patriarchs:
Jesus, master of apostles:
Jesus, teacher of evangelists:
Jesus, strength of martyrs:
Jesus, light of confessors:
Jesus, purity of virgins:
Jesus, crown of all saints:

Psalm 136

The response after each line is:
    For his mercy endures forever.

Give thanks to the Lord, for he is good:
Give thanks to the God of gods:
Give thanks to the Lord of lords:
Who alone does great wonders:
Who made the heavens in wisdom:
Who spread out the earth upon the waters:
Who made the great lights:
The sun to rule over the day:
The moon and the stars to rule over the night:
Who smote the Egyptians in their first-born:
And brought out Israel from their midst:
With a mighty hand and an out-stretched arm:

Who split the Red Sea in twain:
And led Israel through its midst:
But swept Pharaoh and his army into the Red Sea:
Who led his people through the wilderness:
Who smote great kings:
And slew powerful kings:
Sihon, the king of the Amorites:
And Og, king of Bashan:
And made their land a heritage:
The heritage of Israel his servant:
Who remembered us in our abjection:
And freed us from our foes:
Who gives food to all flesh:
Give thanks to the God of heaven:

The invocation "Our Father, our King," is repeated after each line.

Our Father, our King, we have sinned before you.

Our Father, our King, inscribe us for blessing in the book of life.

Our Father, our King, grant us a year of happiness.

Our Father, our King, bestow upon us an abundance of your blessings.

Our Father, our King, have mercy upon us and upon our children.

Our Father, our King, keep far from us sickness, war and famine.

Our Father, our King, banish every oppressor from our midst.

Our Father, our King, bring us back to you in perfect repentance.

Our Father, our King, forgive and pardon all our sins.

Our Father, our King, show us your mercy and your favor.

Our Father, our King, be merciful and answer us.

(From the liturgy of the Day of Atonement)

Prayers of Thanksgiving

Te Deum

This is one of the church's most ancient hymns of praise and thanksgiving.

You are God: we praise you;
You are the Lord: we acclaim you;
You are the eternal Father:
All creation worships you.
To you all angels, all the powers of heaven,
Cherubim and Seraphim, sing in endless praise:
Holy, holy, holy Lord, God of power and might,
heaven and earth are full of your glory.
The glorious company of apostles praise you.
The noble fellowship of prophets praise you.
The white-robed army of martyrs praise you.
Throughout the world the holy Church acclaims you:

Father, of majesty unbounded,
your true and only Son, worthy of all worship,
and the Holy Spirit, advocate and guide.
You, Christ, are the King of glory,
the eternal Son of the Father.
When you became man to set us free
you did not spurn the Virgin's womb.
You overcame the sting of death,
and opened the kingdom of heaven to all believers.
You are seated at God's right hand in glory.
We believe that you will come, and be our judge.
Come then, Lord, and help your people,
bought with the price of your own blood,
and bring us with your saints
to glory everlasting.

Psalm 65:6–14

This is a prayer of thanksgiving for harvest, for the bounty of God.

With awe-inspiring deeds of justice you answer us,
    O God our savior,
The hope of all the ends of the earth
    and of the distant seas.
You set the mountains in place by your power,
    you who are girt with might;
You still the roaring of the seas,
    the roaring of their waves and the tumult of the
        peoples.
And the dwellers at the earth's ends are in fear at your
        marvels;
    the farthest east and west you make resound with joy.
You have visited the land and watered it;
    greatly have you enriched it.
God's watercourses are filled;
    you have prepared the grain.
Thus have you prepared the land: drenching its furrows,
    breaking up its clods.

Softening it with showers,
    blessing its yield.
You have crowned the year with your bounty,
    and your paths overflow with a rich harvest;
The untilled meadows overflow with it,
    and rejoicing clothes the hills.
The fields are garmented with flocks
    and the valleys blanketed with grain.
    They shout and sing for joy.

Psalm 117

Praise the Lord, all you nations;
    glorify him, all you peoples!
For steadfast is his kindness toward us,
    and the fidelity of the Lord endures forever.

Psalm 150

Praise the Lord in his sanctuary,
    praise him in the firmament of his strength.
Priase him for his mighty deeds,
    praise him for his sovereign majesty.
Praise him with the blast of the trumpet,
    praise him with lyre and harp,
Praise him with the timbrel and dance,
    praise him with strings and pipe.
Praise him with sounding cymbals,
    praise him with clanging cymbals.
Let everything that has breath
    praise the Lord! Alleluia.

General Thanksgiving

Let us give thanks to God our Father for all his gifts so
    freely bestowed upon us.
For the beauty and wonder of his creation, in earth and sky
    and sea: we thank you, Lord.
For all that is gracious in the lives of men and women,
    revealing the image of Christ: we thank you, Lord.

For our daily food and drink, our homes and families, and our friends: we thank you, Lord.

For minds to think, and hearts to love, and hands to serve: we thank you, Lord.

For health and strength to work, and leisure to rest and play: we thank you, Lord.

For the brave and courageous, who are patient in suffering and faithful in adversity: we thank you, Lord.

For all valiant seekers after truth, liberty, and justice: we thank you, Lord.

For the communion of saints, in all times and places: we thank you, Lord.

Above all, let us give thanks for the great mercies and promises given to us in Christ Jesus, Our Lord; to him be praise and glory, with the Father and the Holy Spirit, now and for ever. Amen.

(Book of Common Prayer)

Thanksgiving for the Saints and Faithful Departed

We give thanks to you, O Lord our God, for all your servants and witnesses of time past: for Abraham, the father of believers, and Sarah his wife; for Moses, the lawgiver, and Aaron, the priest; for Miriam and Joshua, Deborah and Gideon, and Samuel with Hannah his mother; for Isaiah and all the prophets; for Mary, the mother of our Lord; for Peter and Paul and all the apostles; for Mary and Martha, and Mary Magdalene; for Stephen, the first martyr, and all the martyrs and saints in every age and in every land. In your mercy, O Lord our God, give us, as you gave to them, the hope of salvation and the promise of eternal life; through Jesus Christ our Lord, the first-born of many from the dead. Amen.

Now Thank We All Our God

Now thank we all our God
With heart and hands and voices,
Who wondrous things hath done,
In whom his world rejoices,
Who, from our mothers' arms,
Hath blessed us on our way
With countless gifts of love
And still is ours today.

All praise and thanks to God
The Father now be given,
The Son, and him who reigns
With them in highest heaven,
The one eternal God,
Whom earth and heaven adore,
For thus it was, is now,
And shall be evermore.

(Martin Rinkart)

i thank You God for most this amazing

i thank You God for most this amazing
day:for the leaping greenly spirits of trees
and a blue true dream of sky;and for everything
which is natural which is infinite which is yes

(i who have died am alive again today,
and this is the sun's birthday;this is the birth
day of life and of love and wings:and of the gay
great happening illimitably earth)

how should tasting touching hearing seeing
breathing any—lifted from the no
of all nothing—human merely being
doubt unimaginable You?

(now the ears of my ears awake and
now the eyes of my eyes are opened)

(e. e. cummings)

As If I Asked a Common Alms

As if I asked a common Alms,
And in my wondering hand
A Stranger pressed a Kingdom,
And I, bewildered, stand—
As if I asked the Orient
Had it for me a Morn—
And it should lift its purple Dikes,
And shatter me with Dawn!

(Emily Dickinson)

Devotions

The Rosary*

Praying the Hail Mary over and over, 150 times for the entire rosary, the voice and the mind and the heart can touch on the ways the Lord is present in our lives and history. The decades of the rosary suggest moments in this presence. Each decade begins with the Our Father, then ten Hail Marys, then the Glory Be. Before each set of five decades comes the Apostles' Creed, the Our Father, and three Hail Marys.

Joyful Mysteries

1. *The Annunciation.* "Do not fear, Mary. You have found favor with God. You shall conceive and bear a son and give him the name Jesus. Great will be his dignity and he will be called Son of the Most High." *(Luke 1:30–32)*
2. *The Visitation.* Elizabeth was filled with the Holy Spirit and cried in a loud voice: "Blest are you among women and blest is the fruit of your womb. But who am I that the mother of my Lord should come to me?" *(Luke 1:41–43)*
3. *The Birth of Jesus.* While they were in Bethlehem, the days of Mary's confinement were completed. She gave birth to her first-born son and wrapped him in swaddling clothes and laid him in a manger, because there was no room for them in the place where travelers lodged. *(Luke 2:6–7)*

---

* This meaningful Roman Catholic prayer is included here as representative of a type of devotion in Catholic families. The Angelus which follows is also of this origin.

4. *The Presentation of Jesus.* When the parents brought in the child Jesus to perform for him the customary ritual of the law, Simeon took him in his arms and blessed God in these words: "Now, Master, you can dismiss your servant in peace; you have fulfilled your word. For my eyes have witnessed your saving deed displayed for all the people to see: a revealing light to the Gentiles, the glory of your people Israel." (*Luke 2:27–32*)

5. *The Finding of Jesus in the Temple.* "Son, why have you done this to us? You see that your father and I have been searching for you in sorrow." He said to them: "Why did you search for me? Did you not know I had to be in my Father's house?" And Jesus went home with them and progressed steadily in wisdom and age and grace before God and men. (*Luke 2:48–49, 52*)

Sorrowful Mysteries

1. *The Agony in the Garden.* He kept saying: "Abba, O Father, you have the power to do all things. Take this cup away from me. But let it be as you would have it, not as I." (*Mark 14:36*)

2. *Jesus Is Scourged.* I have not rebelled, have not turned back. I gave my back to those who beat me, my cheeks to those who plucked my beard; my face I did not shield from buffets and spitting. (*Isaiah 50:5–6*)

3. *Jesus Is Crowned with Thorns.* The soldiers dressed him in purple, then wove a crown of thorns and put it on him. Continually striking Jesus on the head with a reed and spitting at him, they genuflected before him and pretended to pay him homage. (*Mark 15:17, 19*)

4. *Jesus Carries the Cross.* When the soldiers had finished mocking him, they stripped him of the purple, dressed him in his own clothes, and led him out to crucify him. (*Mark 15:20*)

5. *Jesus Dies on the Cross.* It was now around midday. Jesus uttered a loud cry and said, "Father, into your hands I commend my spirit." After he said this, he died. (*Luke 23:44, 46*).

Glorious Mysteries

1. *The Resurrection.* He was buried and, in accordance with the scriptures, rose on the third day. He was seen by Cephas, then by the twelve. After that he was seen by five hundred brothers

at once, most of whom are still alive, although some have fallen asleep. Next he was seen by James; then by all the apostles. (*1 Corinthians 15:4–7*)

2. *The Ascension.* Then he led them out near Bethany, and with hands upraised, blessed them. As he blessed, he left them, and was taken up to heaven. They fell down to do him reverence, then returned to Jerusalem filled with joy. There they were to be found in the temple constantly, speaking the praises of God. (*Luke 24:50–53*)

3. *The Coming of the Holy Spirit.* When the day of Pentecost came it found them gathered in one place. Suddenly from up in the sky there came a noise like a strong, driving wind which was heard all through the house where they were seated. All were filled with the Holy Spirit. (*Acts 2:1–2, 4*)

4. *Mary's Assumption.* Stern as death is love, relentless as the nether world is devotion; its flames are a blazing fire. Deep waters cannot quench love, nor floods sweep it away. (*Song of Songs 8:6–7*)

5. *Mary, Queen of Heaven.* You are the glory of Jerusalem, the surpassing joy of Israel; you are the splendid boast of our people. May you be blessed by the Lord almighty forever and ever. (*Judith 15:9–10*)

The Angelus
This prayer is traditionally recited three times a day: early in the morning, at noon, and in the evening. Like other forms of morning and evening prayer, the angelus is a way to fashion the praise of God from time itself. It ponders the incarnation, the wonder of the Lord present in creation. If the angelus is prayed standing up, it is customary to genuflect on the words: "And the word became flesh and dwelt among us."

> The angel of the Lord declared unto Mary;
>   And she conceived of the Holy Spirit.
>   Hail Mary . . .
> Behold the handmaid of the Lord;

Be it done unto me according to your word.
Hail Mary . . .
And the word was made flesh;
And dwelled among us.
Hail Mary . . .
Pray for us, O holy mother of God:
That we may be made worthy of the promises of
Christ.
Let us pray. Pour forth, we beseech you, O Lord, your
grace into our hearts,
that we, to whom the incarnation of Christ your Son
was made known by the message of an angel,
may be brought, by his passion and cross, to the glory of his
resurrection.
We ask this through the same Christ our Lord. Amen.

Blessings

To bless is to give praise and thanks. It is to extend something of
oneself into that which is being blessed. That is why the blessing
is often accompanied by a gesture of touching, laying on of
hands, or by the extending of hands toward or over the person
or the object being blessed. Many blessings are used in the
various sections of this book. What follows are some not included earlier.

May grace and peace from God our Father, and Christ
Jesus our Savior, be with you. (*Titus 1:4*)

Favor and peace be yours in abundance. (*1 Peter 1:2*)

May he who is the Lord of peace give you continued peace
in every possible way. (*2 Thessalonians 3:16*)

The Lord be with you all. (*2 Thessalonians 3:16*)

Blessed is your glorious name and exalted above all blessing and praise. (*Nehemiah 9:5*)

Blessed be God, and praised be his great name,
    and blessed be all his holy angels.
May his holy name be praised
    throughout all the ages.

(Tobit 11:14)

Various Prayers

The Lord's Prayer (Traditional)
Our Father, who art in heaven,
hallowed be thy name.
Thy kingdom come.
Thy will be done on earth as it is in heaven.
Give us this day our daily bread,
and forgive us our trespasses
as we forgive those who trespass against us.
And lead us not into temptation
but deliver us from evil.
(*Doxology*) For thine is the kingdom,
        and the power, and the glory,
        forever and ever. Amen.

The Lord's Prayer (Common translation)
Our Father in heaven,
hallowed be your name,
your kingdom come,
your will be done, on earth as in heaven.
Give us today our daily bread.
Forgive us our sins
as we forgive those who sin against us.
Save us from the time of trial,
and deliver us from evil.
(*Doxology*) For the kingdom, the power,
        and the glory are yours,
        now and for ever. Amen.

The Apostles' Creed

I believe in God,
    the Father almighty,
    creator of heaven and earth.
I believe in Jesus Christ, his only Son, our Lord.
    He was conceived by the power of the Holy Spirit
    and born of the virgin Mary.
    He suffered under Pontius Pilate,
    was crucified, died, and was buried.
    He descended to the dead.
    On the third day he rose again.
    He ascended into heaven,
    and is seated at the right hand of the Father.
    He will come again to judge the living and the dead.
I believe in the Holy Spirit,
    the holy catholic church,
    the communion of saints,
    the forgiveness of sins,
    the resurrection of the body,
    and life everlasting.

The Nicene Creed

We believe in one God,
    the Father, the almighty,
    maker of heaven and earth,
    of all that is seen and unseen.
We believe in one Lord, Jesus Christ,
    the only Son of God,
    eternally begotten of the Father,
    God from God, Light from Light,
    true God from true God,
    begotten, not made, one in Being with the Father.
    Through him all things were made.
    For us and for our salvation
    he came down from heaven:
    by the power of the Holy Spirit
    he was born of the virgin Mary, and became man.

For our sake he was crucified under Pontius Pilate;
he suffered, died, and was buried.
On the third day he rose again
in fulfillment of the scriptures;
he ascended into heaven
and is seated at the right hand of the Father.
He will come again in glory to judge the living and the
dead,
and his kingdom will have no end.
We believe in the Holy Spirit, the Lord, the giver of life,
who proceeds from the Father and the Son.
With the Father and the Son he is worshiped and
glorified.
He has spoken through the prophets.
We believe in one, holy, catholic and apostolic Church.
We acknowledge one baptism for the forgiveness of
sins.
We look for the resurrection of the dead,
and the life of the world to come. Amen.

The Gloria

Glory to God in the highest,
and peace to his people on earth.
Lord God, heavenly King,
almighty God and Father,
we worship you, we give you thanks,
we praise you for your glory.
Lord Jesus Christ, only Son of the Father,
Lord God, Lamb of God,
you take away the sin of the world: have mercy on us;
you are seated at the right hand of the Father: receive our
prayer.
For you alone are the Holy One,
you alone are the Lord,
you alone are the Most High, Jesus Christ,
with the Holy Spirit, in the glory of God the Father.
Amen.

The Hail Mary

Hail, Mary, full of grace:
the Lord is with you.
Blessed are you among women
and blessed is the fruit of your womb, Jesus.
Holy Mary, mother of God,
pray for us sinners now and at the hour of our death.
Amen.

Appendix I

SCRIPTURES FOR SUNDAYS AND FEASTS

In several instances, the scripture reference given here will not be exactly the same as that found in the Sunday lectionary for the liturgy. The latter will be a more careful rendering of the scripture, often omitting verses that are out of place or confusing. But since this would be difficult to do when reading from the Bible at home, many of these references have been simplified.

The psalm reference for each Sunday is usually to the psalm used for reflection in the liturgy between the first and second readings. No verse references are given here, partly because of limitations of space: the psalm verses selected for the liturgy often skip around through the psalm. Often this psalm will contain a few verses that could be used as a prayer on Sunday and through the week.

All Sundays of the year have been included in the list and most of the festivals which may replace the Sundays: Christmas; Mary, Mother of God, Name Day (January 1); Assumption (August 15); All Saints (November 1); Immaculate Conception (December 8).

The lessons which follow are those found in the Roman Catholic Church. This three-year cycle of lessons is also followed with some variations by Lutherans and Episcopalians. These variations can be checked with the calendars as found in the *Lutheran Book of Worship* or *The Book of Common Prayer*. Increasingly, other churches as well are using this three-year lectionary system.

Sunday	First Reading	Second Reading	Third Reading
1 Advent-A			
Psalm 122	Is 5:1–5	Rom 13:11–14	Mt 24:37–44
1 Advent-B			
Psalm 80	Is 63:16–19; 64:2–7	1 Cor 1:3–9	Mk 13:33–37
1 Advent-C			
Psalm 25	Jer 33:14–16	1 Thes 3:12–4:2	Lk 21:25–28, 34–36
2 Advent-A			
Psalm 72	Is 11:1–10	Rom 15:4–9	Mt 3:1–12
2 Advent-B			
Psalm 85	Is 40:1–5, 9–11	2 Pet 3:8–14	Mk 1:1–8
2 Advent-C			
Psalm 126	Bar 5:1–9	Phil 1:4–7, 8–11	Lk 3:1–6
3 Advent-A			
Psalm 146	Is 34:1–6, 10	Jas 5:7–10	Mt 11:2–11
3 Advent-B			
Lk 1:46–54	Is 61:1–2, 10–11	1 Thes 5:16–24	Jn 1:6–8, 19–28
3 Advent-C			
Is 12:2–6	Zep 3:14–18	Phil 4:4–7	Lk 3:10–18
4 Advent-A			
Psalm 24	Is 7:10–14	Rom 1:1–7	Mt 1:18–25
4 Advent-B			
Psalm 89	2 Sm 7:1–5, 8–16	Rom 16:25–27	Lk 1:26–38
4 Advent-C			
Psalm 80	Mi 5:1–4	Heb 10:5–10	Lk 1:39–45
Christmas:			
Midnight	Is 9:1–6	Ti 2:11–14	Lk 2:1–14
Dawn	Is 62:11–12	Ti 3:4–7	Lk 2:15–20
Day	Is 52:7–10	Heb 1:1–6	Jn 1:1–18
Psalm 96			
Holy Family-A			
Psalm 128	Sir 3:2–6, 12–14	Col 3:12–21	Mt 2:13–15, 19–23
Holy Family-B			
Psalm 128	Sir 3:2–6, 12–14	Col 3:12–21	Lk 2:41–52
Holy Family-C			
Psalm 128	Sir 3:2–6, 12–14	Col 3:12–21	Lk 2:41–52
Mary, Mother of God (Name Day)			
Psalm 67	Nm 6:22–27	Gal 4:4–7	Lk 2:16–21
Epiphany			
Psalm 72	Is 60:1–6	Eph 3:2–6	Mt 2:1–12

Sunday	First Reading	Second Reading	Third Reading
Baptism of the Lord-A			
Psalm 29	Is 42:1–7	Acts 10:34–38	Mt 3:13–17
Baptism of the Lord-B			
Psalm 29	Is 42:1–7	Acts 10:34–38	Mt 1:7–11
Baptism of the Lord-C			
Psalm 29	Is 42:1–7	Acts 10:34–38	Lk 3:15–16, 21–22
1 Lent-A			
Psalm 51	Gn 2:7–9; 3:1–7	Rom 5:12–19	Mt 4:1–11
1 Lent-B			
Psalm 25	Gn 9:8–15	1 Pt 3:18–22	Mk 1:12–15
1 Lent-C			
Psalm 91	Dt 26:4–10	Rom 10:8–13	Lk 4:1–13
2 Lent-A			
Psalm 33	Gn 12:1–4	2 Tim 1:8–10	Mt 17:1–9
2 Lent-B			
Psalm 116	Gn 22:1–2, 9–18	Rom 8:31–34	Mk 9:1–10
2 Lent-C			
Psalm 27	Gn 15:5–12, 17–18	Phil 3:17—4:1	Lk 9:28–36
3 Lent-A			
Psalm 95	Ex 17:3–7	Rom 5:1–2, 5–8	Jn 4:5–42
3 Lent-B			
Psalm 19	Ex 20:1–17	1 Cor 1:22–25	Jn 2:13–25
3 Lent-C			
Psalm 103	Ex 3:1–8, 13–15	1 Cor 10:1–6, 10–12	Lk 13:1–9 (or Jn 4:5–42)
4 Lent-A			
Psalm 23	1 Sm 16:1, 6–7, 10–13	Eph 5:8–14	Jn 9:1–41
4 Lent-B			
Psalm 137	2 Chr 36:14–23	Eph 2:4–10	Jn 3:14–21 (or Jn 9:1–41)
4 Lent-C			
Psalm 34	Jos 5:9–12	2 Cor 5:17–21	Lk 15:1–3, 11–32 (or Jn 9:1–41)
5 Lent-A			
Psalm 130	Ez 37:12–14	Rom 8:8–11	Jn 11:1–45
5 Lent-B			
Psalm 51	Jer 31:31–34	Heb 5:7–9	Jn 12:20–33 (or Jn 11:1–45)

Sunday	First Reading	Second Reading	Third Reading
5 Lent-C			
Psalm 126	Is 43:16–21	Phil 3:8–14	Jn 8:1–11 (or Jn 11:1–45)
Passion Sunday-A			
Psalm 22	Is 50:4–7	Phil 2:6–11	Mt 27:11–54
Passion Sunday-B			
Psalm 22	Is 50:4–7	Phil 2:6–11	Mk 15:1–39
Passion Sunday-C			
Psalm 22	Is 50:4–7	Phil 2:6–11	Lk 23:1–49
Easter Sunday-A			
Psalm 118	Acts 10:34–43	Col 3:1–4	Mt 28:1–10
Easter Sunday-B			
Psalm 118	Acts 10:34–43	Col 3:1–4	Mk 16:1–8
Easter Sunday-C			
Psalm 118	Acts 10:34–43	Col 3:1–4	Lk 24:1–12
2 Easter-A			
Psalm 118	Acts 2:42–47	1 Pt 1:3–9	Jn 20:19–31
2 Easter-B			
Psalm 118	Acts 4:32–35	1 Jn 5:1–6	Jn 20:19–31
2 Easter-C			
Psalm 118	Acts 5:12–16	Rev 1:9–13, 17–19	Jn 20:19–31
3 Easter-A			
Psalm 16	Acts 2:14, 22–28	1 Pt 1:17–21	Lk 24:13–35
3 Easter-B			
Psalm 14	Acts 3:13–19	1 Jn 2:1–5	Lk 24:35–48
3 Easter-C			
Psalm 30	Acts 5:27–32, 40–41	Rev 5:11–14	Jn 21:1–19
4 Easter-A			
Psalm 23	Acts 2:14, 36–41	1 Pt 2:20–25	Jn 10:1–10
4 Easter-B			
Psalm 118	Acts 4:8–12	1 Jn 3:1–2	Jn 10:11–18
4 Easter-C			
Psalm 100	Acts 13:14, 43–52	Rev 7:9, 14–17	Jn 10:27–30
5 Easter-A			
Psalm 33	Acts 6:1–7	1 Pt 2:4–9	Jn 14:1–12
5 Easter-B			
Psalm 22	Acts 9:26–31	1 Jn 3:18–24	Jn 15:1–8
5 Easter-C			
Psalm 145	Acts 14:21–27	Rev 21:1–5	Jn 13:31–35

Sunday	First Reading	Second Reading	Third Reading
6 Easter-A			
Psalm 67	Acts 8:5–8, 14–17	1 Pt 3:15–18	Jn 14:15–21
6 Easter-B			
Psalm 98	Acts 10:25–26, 34–35, 44–48	1 Jn 4:7–10	Jn 15:9–17
6 Easter-C			
Psalm 67	Acts 15:1–2, 22–29	Rev 21:10–14, 22–23	Jn 14:23–29
7 Easter-A			
Psalm 27	Acts 1:12–14	1 Pt 4:13–16	Jn 17:1–11
7 Easter-B			
Psalm 103	Acts 1:15–17, 20–26	1 Jn 4:11–16	Jn 17:11–19
7 Easter-C			
Psalm 97	Acts 7:55–60	Rev 22:12–14, 16–17, 20	Jn 17:20–26
Pentecost			
Psalm 104	Acts 2:1–11	1 Cor 12:3–7, 12–13	Jn 20:19–23
Trinity Sunday-A			
Daniel 3	Ex 34:4–9	2 Cor 13:11–13	Jn 3:16–18
Trinity Sunday-B			
Psalm 33	Dt 4:32–34, 39–40	Rom 8:14–17	Mt 28:16–20
Trinity Sunday-C			
Psalm 8	Prv 8:22–31	Rom 5:1–5	Jn 16:12–15
Corpus Christi-A			
Psalm 147	Dt 8:2–3, 14–16	1 Cor 10:16–17	Jn 6:51–59
Corpus Christi-B			
Psalm 116	Ex 24:3–8	Heb 9:11–15	Mk 14:12–16, 22–26
Corpus Christi-C			
Psalm 110	Gn 14:18–20	1 Cor 11:23–26	Lk 9:11–17
2 Ordinary Time-A			
Psalm 40	Is 49:3–6	1 Cor 1:1–3	Jn 1:29–34
2 Ordinary Time-B			
Psalm 40	1 Sm 3:3–10, 19	1 Cor 6:13–20	Jn 1:35–42
2 Ordinary Time-C			
Psalm 96	Is 62:1–5	1 Cor 12:4–11	Jn 2:1–12
3 Ordinary Time-A			
Psalm 27	Is 8:23—9:3	1 Cor 1:10–13, 17	Mt 4:12–23

Sunday	First Reading	Second Reading	Third Reading
3 Ordinary Time-B			
Psalm 25	Jon 3:1–5, 10	1 Cor 7:29–31	Mk 1:14–20
3 Ordinary Time-C			
Psalm 19	Neh 8:2–10	1 Cor 12:12–30	Lk 1:1–4; 4:14–21
4 Ordinary Time-A			
Psalm 146	Zep 2:3; 3:12–13	1 Cor 1:26–31	Mt 5:1–12
4 Ordinary Time-B			
Psalm 95	Dt 18:15–20	1 Cor 7:32–35	Mk 1:21–28
4 Ordinary Time-C			
Psalm 71	Jer 1:4–5, 17–19	1 Cor 13:4–13	Lk 4:21–30
5 Ordinary Time-A			
Psalm 112	Is 58:7–10	1 Cor 2:1–5	Mt 5:13–16
5 Ordinary Time-B			
Psalm 147	Jb 7:1–7	1 Cor 9:16–19, 22–23	Mk 1:29–39
5 Ordinary Time-C			
Psalm 138	Is 6:1–8	1 Cor 15:1–11	Lk 5:1–11
6 Ordinary Time-A			
Psalm 119	Sir 15:15–20	1 Cor 2:6–10	Mt 5:17–37
6 Ordinary Time-B			
Psalm 32	Lv 13:1–2, 44–46	1 Cor 10:31—11:1	Mk 1:40–45
6 Ordinary Time-C			
Psalm 1	Jer 17:5–8	1 Cor 15:12, 16–20	Lk 6:17, 20–26
7 Ordinary Time-A			
Psalm 103	Lv 19:1–2, 17–18	1 Cor 3:16–23	Mt 5:38–48
7 Ordinary Time-B			
Psalm 41	Is 43:18–25	2 Cor 1:18–22	Mk 2:1–12
7 Ordinary Time-C			
Psalm 103	1 Sm 26:2, 7–13, 22–23	1 Cor 15:45–49	Lk 6:27–38
8 Ordinary Time-A			
Psalm 62	Is 49:14–15	1 Cor 4:1–5	Mt 6:24–34
8 Ordinary Time-B			
Psalm 103	Hos 2:16–17, 21–22	2 Cor 3:1–6	Mk 2:18–22
8 Ordinary Time-C			
Psalm 92	Sir 27:4–7	1 Cor 15:54–58	Lk 6:39–45
9 Ordinary Time-A			
Psalm 31	Dt 11:18, 26–28	Rom 3:21–25, 28	Mt 7:21–27

Sunday	First Reading	Second Reading	Third Reading
9 Ordinary Time-B			
Psalm 81	Dt 5:12–15	2 Cor 4:6–11	Mk 2:23—3:6
9 Ordinary Time-C			
Psalm 117	1 Kgs 8:41–43	Gal 1:1–2, 6–10	Lk 7:1–10
10 Ordinary Time-A			
Psalm 50	Hos 6:3–6	Rom 4:18–25	Mt 9:9–13
10 Ordinary Time-B			
Psalm 130	Gn 3:9–15	2 Cor 4:13—5:1	Mk 3:20–35
10 Ordinary Time-C			
Psalm 130	1 Kgs 17:17–24	Gal 1:11–19	Lk 7:11–17
11 Ordinary Time-A			
Psalm 100	Ex 19:2–6	Rom 5:6–11	Mt 9:36—10:8
11 Ordinary Time-B			
Psalm 92	Ez 17:22–24	2 Cor 5:6–10	Mk 4:26–34
11 Ordinary Time-C			
Psalm 32	2 Sam 12:7–10, 13	Gal 2:16, 19–21	Lk 7:36—8:3
12 Ordinary Time-A			
Psalm 69	Jer 20:10–13	Rom 5:12–15	Mt 10:26–33
12 Ordinary Time-B			
Psalm 107	Jb 38:1, 8–11	2 Cor 5:14–17	Mk 4:35–41
12 Ordinary Time-C			
Psalm 63	Zec 12:10–11	Gal 3:26–29	Lk 9:18–24
13 Ordinary Time-A			
Psalm 89	2 Kgs 4:8–11, 14–16	Rom 6:3–4, 8–11	Mt 10:37–42
13 Ordinary Time-B			
Psalm 30	Wis 1:13–15; 2:23–24	2 Cor 8:7–9, 13–15	Mk 5:21–43
13 Ordinary Time-C			
Psalm 16	1 Kgs 19:16, 19–21	Gal 5:1, 13–18	Lk 9:51–62
14 Ordinary Time-A			
Psalm 145	Zec 9:9–10	Rom 8:9–13	Mt 11:25–30
14 Ordinary Time-B			
Psalm 123	Ez 2:2–5	2 Cor 12:7–10	Mk 6:1–6
14 Ordinary Time-C			
Psalm 66	Is 66:10–14	Gal 6:14–18	Lk 10:1–12, 17–20
15 Ordinary Time-A			
Psalm 65	Is 55:10–11	Rom 8:18, 23	Mt 13:1–23
15 Ordinary Time-B			
Psalm 85	Am 7:12–15	Eph 1:3–14	Mk 6:7–13

Sunday	First Reading	Second Reading	Third Reading
15 Ordinary Time-C			
Psalm 69	Dt 30:10–14	Col 1:15–20	Lk 10:25–37
16 Ordinary Time-A			
Psalm 86	Wis 12:13, 16–19	Rom 8:26–27	Mt 13:24–43
16 Ordinary Time-B			
Psalm 23	Jer 23:1–6	Eph 2:13–18	Mk 6:30–34
16 Ordinary Time-C			
Psalm 15	Gn 18:1–10	Col 1:24–28	Lk 10:38–42
17 Ordinary Time-A			
Psalm 119	1 Kgs 3:5, 7–12	Rom 8:28–30	Mt 13:44–52
17 Ordinary Time-B			
Psalm 145	2 Kgs 4:42–44	Eph 4:1–6	Jn 6:1–15
17 Ordinary Time-C			
Psalm 138	Gn 18:20–32	Col 2:12–14	Lk 11:1–13
18 Ordinary Time-A			
Psalm 145	Is 55:1–3	Rom 8:35–39	Mt 14:13–21
18 Ordinary Time-B			
Psalm 78	Ex 16:2–4, 12–15	Eph 4:17, 20–24	Jn 6:24–35
18 Ordinary Time-C			
Psalm 95	Ecc 1:2; 2:21–23	Col 3:1–5, 9–11	Lk 12:13–21
19 Ordinary Time-A			
Psalm 85	1 Kgs 19:9–13	Rom 9:1–5	Mt 14:22–33
19 Ordinary Time-B			
Psalm 34	1 Kgs 19:4–8	Eph 4:30—5:2	Jn 6:41–51
19 Ordinary Time-C			
Psalm 33	Wis 18:6–9	Heb 11:1–2, 8–19	Lk 12:32–48
20 Ordinary Time-A			
Psalm 67	Is 56:1, 6–7	Rom 11:13–15, 29–32	Mt 15:21–28
20 Ordinary Time-B			
Psalm 34	Prv 9:1–6	Eph 5:15–20	Jn 6:51–58
20 Ordinary Time-C			
Psalm 40	Jer 38:4–10	Heb 12:1–4	Lk 12:49–53
21 Ordinary Time-A			
Psalm 138	Is 22:19–23	Rom 11:33–36	Mt 16:13–20
21 Ordinary Time-B			
Psalm 34	Jos 24:1–2, 15–18	Eph 5:21–32	Jn 6:60–69
21 Ordinary Time-C			
Psalm 117	Is 66:18–21	Heb 12:5–7, 11–13	Lk 13:22–30
22 Ordinary Time-A			
Psalm 63	Jer 20:7–9	Rom 12:1–2	Mt 16:21–27

Sunday	First Reading	Second Reading	Third Reading
22 Ordinary Time-B			
Psalm 15	Dt 4:1–2, 6–8	Jas 1:17–18, 21–22, 27	Mk 7:1–8, 14–15, 21–23
22 Ordinary Time-C			
Psalm 68	Sir 3:17–20, 28–29	Heb 12:18–19, 22–24	Lk 14:1, 7–14
23 Ordinary Time-A			
Psalm 95	Ez 33:7–9	Rom 13:8–10	Mt 18:15–20
23 Ordinary Time-B			
Psalm 146	Is 35:4–7	Jas 2:1–5	Mk 7:31–37
23 Ordinary Time-C			
Psalm 90	Wis 9:13–19	Phlm 9—17	Lk 14:25–35
24 Ordinary Time-A			
Psalm 103	Sir 27:30—28:7	Rom 14:7–9	Mt 18:21–35
24 Ordinary Time-B			
Psalm 116	Is 50:4–9	Jas 2:14–18	Mk 8:27–35
24 Ordinary Time-C			
Psalm 51	Ex 32:7–14	1 Tim 1:12–17	Lk 15:1–32
25 Ordinary Time-A			
Psalm 145	Is 55:6–9	Phil 1:20–24, 27	Mt 20:1–16
25 Ordinary Time-B			
Psalm 54	Wis 2:12, 17–20	Jas 3:16—4:3	Mk 9:30–37
25 Ordinary Time-C			
Psalm 113	Am 8:4–7	1 Tim 2:1–8	Lk 16:1–13
26 Ordinary Time-A			
Psalm 125	Ez 18:25–28	Phil 2:1–11	Mt 21:28–32
26 Ordinary Time-B			
Psalm 19	Nm 11:25–29	Jas 5:1–6	Mk 9:38–48
26 Ordinary Time-C			
Psalm 146	Am 6:1, 4–7	1 Tim 6:11–16	Lk 16:19–31
27 Ordinary Time-A			
Psalm 80	Is 5:1–7	Phil 4:6–9	Mt 21:33–43
27 Ordinary Time-B			
Psalm 128	Gn 2:18–24	Heb 2:9–11	Mk 10:2–16
27 Ordinary Time-C			
Psalm 95	Hb 1:2–3; 2:2–4	2 Tim 1:6–8, 13–14	Lk 17:5–10
28 Ordinary Time-A			
Psalm 23	Is 25:6–10	Phil 4:12–14, 19–20	Mt 22:1–14
28 Ordinary Time-B			
Psalm 90	Ws 7:7–11	Heb 4:12–13	Mk 10:17–30

Sunday	First Reading	Second Reading	Third Reading
28 Ordinary Time-C			
Psalm 98	2 Kgs 5:14–17	2 Tim 2:8–13	Lk 17:11–19
29 Ordinary Time-A			
Psalm 96	Is 45:1, 4–6	1 Thes 1:1–5	Mt 22:15–21
29 Ordinary Time-B			
Psalm 33	Is 53:10–11	Heb 4:14–16	Mk 10:35–45
29 Ordinary Time-C			
Psalm 121	Ex 17:8–13	2 Tim 3:14—4:2	Lk 18:1–8
30 Ordinary Time-A			
Psalm 18	Ex 22:20–26	1 Thes 1:5–10	Mt 22:34–40
30 Ordinary Time-B			
Psalm 126	Jer 31:7–9	Heb 5:1–6	Mk 10:46–52
30 Ordinary Time-C			
Psalm 34	Sir 35:12–18	2 Tim 4:6–8, 16–18	Lk 18:9–14
31 Ordinary Time-A			
Psalm 131	Mal 1:14—2:2, 8–10	1 Thes 2:7–9, 13	Mt 23:1–12
31 Ordinary Time-B			
Psalm 18	Dt 6:2–6	Heb 7:23–28	Mk 12:28–34
31 Ordinary Time-C			
Psalm 145	Wis 11:23—12:2	2 Thes 1:11—2:2	Lk 19:1–10
32 Ordinary Time-A			
Psalm 63	Wis 6:12–18	1 Thes 4:13–18	Mt 25:1–13
32 Ordinary Time-B			
Psalm 146	1 Kgs 17:10–16	Heb 9:24–28	Mk 12:38–44
32 Ordinary Time-C			
Psalm 17	2 Mc 7:1–2, 9–14	2 Thes 2:16—3:5	Lk 20:27–38
33 Ordinary Time-A			
Psalm 128	Prv 31:10–13, 19–20, 30–31	1 Thes 5:1–6	Mt 25:14–30
33 Ordinary Time-B			
Psalm 16	Dn 12:1–3	Heb 10:11–14, 18	Mk 13:24–32
33 Ordinary Time-C			
Psalm 98	Mal 3:19–20	2 Thes 3:7–12	Lk 21:5–19
Christ the King-A			
Psalm 23	Ez 34:11–12, 15–17	1 Cor 15:20–26, 28	Mt 25:31–46
Christ the King-B			
Psalm 93	Dn 7:13–14	Rev 1:5–8	Jn 18:33–37
Christ the King-C			
Psalm 122	2 Sam 5:1–3	Col 1:12–20	Lk 23:35–43

Sunday	First Reading	Second Reading	Third Reading
Assumption			
Psalm 45	Rev 11:19; 12:1–6, 10	1 Cor 15:20–26	Lk 1:39–56
All Saints			
Psalm 24	Rev 7:2–4, 9–14	1 Jn 3:1–3	Mt 5:1–12
Immaculate Conception			
Psalm 98	Gn 3:9–15, 20	Eph 1:3–6, 11–12	Lk 1:26–38

Appendix II

SCRIPTURES FOR WEEKDAYS OF ORDINARY TIME

Throughout this book families are encouraged to read a portion of scripture as a part of every day's period of worship either together or separately. In the sections devoted to Advent, Christmas, Lent, and Easter daily readings have been listed with the hope that families would begin especially at these times the practice of daily reading of scripture.

Because the readings for other times of the year, or "ordinary time," as well as the terminology used to describe these times vary somewhat between churches, it is suggested that each individual or family using this book consult the daily lectionary published by his or her church. Such daily lectionaries are now a part of at least two new books in use by parts of Christendom: *The Book of Common Prayer* (1977) and the *Lutheran Book of Worship* (1978).

In addition to the use of these lectionaries, families will want to plan their own systems of daily readings, perhaps reading through various books of the Bible at the individual's or the group's own pace. Whatever lectionary or system is used, the practice of daily reading of scripture on a planned basis will greatly enrich the devotional life of the individual or family.

For those who want to begin daily readings and do not have access to one of the lectionaries mentioned above, the following readings from the lectionary of the Roman Catholic Church are suggested. Additional readings are available but those listed here for ordinary time are one of the readings from one of the years in the lectionary. The weekdays of ordinary time come between the second Sunday in January and Ash Wednesday, and between Pentecost Sunday and the First Sunday in Advent. Because of the variations in the time of Easter, of course, these weeks will not always correspond with the same numbers. Scriptures for the Sundays are listed in Appendix I. A key to the abbreviations of the books of scripture follows the list.

First Week		*Second Week*	
Monday	1 Sm 1:1–8	Monday	1 Sm 15:16–23
Tuesday	1 Sm 1:9–20	Tuesday	1 Sm 16:1–13
Wednesday	1 Sm 3:1–10, 19–20	Wednesday	1 Sm 17:32–51
		Thursday	1 Sm 18:6–9; 19:1–7
Thursday	1 Sm 4:1–11		
Friday	1 Sm 8:4–7, 10–22	Friday	1 Sm 24:3–21
		Saturday	2 Sm 1:1–27
Saturday	1 Sm 9:1–4, 17–19; 10:1		

Third Week		*Fourth Week*	
Monday	2 Sm 5:1–7, 10	Monday	2 Sm 15:13–14; 30:16:5–13
Tuesday	2 Sm 6:12–19		
Wednesday	2 Sm 7:4–17	Tuesday	2 Sm 18:9–19:3
Thursday	2 Sm 7:18–19, 24–29	Wednesday	1 Sm 24:2, 9–17
		Thursday	1 Kgs 2:1–4, 10–12
Friday	2 Sm 11:1–17		
Saturday	2 Sm 12:1–7, 10–17	Friday	Sir 47:2–11
		Saturday	1 Kgs 3:4–13

Fifth Week		*Sixth Week*	
Monday	1 Kgs 8:1–13	Monday	Jas 1:1–11
Tuesday	1 Kgs 8:22–30	Tuesday	Jas 1:12–18
Wednesday	1 Kgs 10:1–10	Wednesday	Jas 1:19–27
Thursday	1 Kgs 11:4–13	Thursday	Jas 2:1–9
Friday	1 Kgs 11:29–32; 12:19	Friday	Jas 2:14–26
		Saturday	Jas 3:1–10
Saturday	1 Kgs 12:26–32; 13:33–34		

Seventh Week		Eighth Week	
Monday	Jas 3:13–18	Monday	1 Pt 1:3–9
Tuesday	Jas 4:1–10	Tuesday	1 Pt 1:10–16
Wednesday	Jas 4:13–17	Wednesday	1 Pt 1:18–25
Thursday	Jas 5:1–6	Thursday	1 Pt 2:2–5, 9–12
Friday	Jas 5:9–12	Friday	1 Pt 4:7–13
Saturday	Jas 5:13–20	Saturday	Jude 17:20–25

Ninth Week		Tenth Week	
Monday	2 Pt 1:2–7	Monday	1 Kgs 17:1–6
Tuesday	2 Pt 3:12–18	Tuesday	1 Kgs 17:7–16
Wednesday	2 Tm 1:1–3, 6–12	Wednesday	1 Kgs 18:20–39
Thursday	2 Tm 2:8–15	Thursday	1 Kgs 18:41–46
Friday	2 Tm 3:10–17	Friday	1 Kgs 19:9–16
Saturday	2 Tm 4:1–8	Saturday	1 Kgs 19:19–21

Eleventh Week		Twelfth Week	
Monday	1 Kgs 21:1–16	Monday	2 Kgs 17:5–8, 13–18
Tuesday	1 Kgs 21:17–29		
Wednesday	2 Kgs 2:1, 6–14	Tuesday	2 Kgs 19:9–21, 31–36
Thursday	Sir 48:1–14		
Friday	2 Kgs 11:1–4, 9–20	Wednesday	2 Kgs 22:8–13; 23:1–3
Saturday	2 Chr 24:17–25	Thursday	2 Kgs 24:8–17
		Friday	2 Kgs 25:1–12
		Saturday	Lam 2:2, 10–14, 18–19

Thirteenth Week		Fourteenth Week	
Monday	Am 2:6–16	Monday	Hos 2:16–18, 21–22
Tuesday	Am 3:1–8; 4:11, 12		
		Tuesday	Hos 8:4–7, 11–13
Wednesday	Am 5:14–15, 21–24	Wednesday	Hos 10:1–3, 7–8, 12
Thursday	Am 7:10–17	Thursday	Hos 11:1, 3–4, 8–9
Friday	Am 8:4–12		
Saturday	Am 9:11–15	Friday	Hos 14:2–10
		Saturday	Is 6:1–8

Fifteenth Week		*Sixteenth Week*	
Monday	Is 1:10–17	Monday	Mi 6:1–8
Tuesday	Is 7:1–9	Tuesday	Mi 7:14–15,
Wednesday	Is 10:5–7, 13–16		18–20
Thursday	Is 26:7–9, 12,	Wednesday	Jer 1:1, 4–10
	16–19	Thursday	Jer 2:1–3, 7–8,
Friday	Is 38:1–6		12–13
Saturday	Mi 2:1–5	Friday	Jer 3:14–17
		Saturday	Jer 7:1–11

Seventeenth Week		*Eighteenth Week*	
Monday	Jer 13:1–11	Monday	Jer 28:1–17
Tuesday	Jer 14:17–22	Tuesday	Jer 30:1–2,
Wednesday	Jer 15:10, 16–21		12–15, 18–22
Thursday	Jer 18:1–6	Wednesday	Jer 31:1–7
Friday	Jer 26:1–9	Thursday	Jer 31:31–34
Saturday	Jer 26:11–16, 24	Friday	Na 2:1–3; 3:1–7
		Saturday	Hb 1:12—2:4

Nineteenth Week		*Twentieth Week*	
Monday	Ez 1:2–5, 24–28	Monday	Ez 24:15–24
Tuesday	Ez 2:8—3:4	Tuesday	Ez 28:1–10
Wednesday	Ez 9:1–10, 18–22	Wednesday	Ez 34:1–11
Thursday	Ez 12:1–2	Thursday	Ez 36:23–28
Friday	Ez 16:1–15, 60,	Friday	Ez 37:1–17
	63	Saturday	Ez 43:1–7
Saturday	Ez 18:1–10, 13,		
	30–32		

Twenty-First Week		*Twenty-Second Week*	
Monday	2 Thes 1:1–5,	Monday	1 Cor 2:1–5
	11–12	Tuesday	1 Cor 2:10–16
Tuesday	2 Thes 2:1–3,	Wednesday	1 Cor 3:1–9
	14–16	Thursday	1 Cor 3:18–23
Wednesday	2 Thes 3:6–10,	Friday	1 Cor 4:1–5
	16–18	Saturday	1 Cor 4:9–15
Thursday	1 Cor 1:1–9		
Friday	1 Cor 1:17–25		
Saturday	1 Cor 1:26–31		

Twenty-Third Week

Monday	1 Cor 5:1–8
Tuesday	1 Cor 6:1–11
Wednesday	1 Cor 7:25–31
Thursday	1 Cor 8:1–7, 11–13
Friday	1 Cor 9:16–19, 22–27
Saturday	1 Cor 10:14–22

Twenty-Fourth Week

Monday	1 Cor 11:17–26, 33
Tuesday	1 Cor 12:12–14, 27–31
Wednesday	1 Cor 12:31— 13:13
Thursday	1 Cor 15:1–11
Friday	1 Cor 15:12–20
Saturday	1 Cor 15:35–37, 42–49

Twenty-Fifth Week

Monday	Prv 3:27–34
Tuesday	Prv 21:1–6, 10–13
Wednesday	Prv 30:5–9
Thursday	Eccl 1:2–11
Friday	Eccl 3:1–11
Saturday	Eccl 11:9—12:8

Twenty-Sixth Week

Monday	Jb 1:6–22
Tuesday	Jb 3:1–3, 11–23
Wednesday	Jb 9:1–16
Thursday	Jb 19:21–27
Friday	Jb 38:12–21; 40:3–5
Saturday	Jb 42:1–6, 12–16

Twenty-Seventh Week

Monday	Gal 1:6–12
Tuesday	Gal 1:13–24
Wednesday	Gal 2:1–2, 7–14
Thursday	Gal 3:1–5
Friday	Gal 3:7–14
Saturday	Gal 3:22–29

Twenty-Eighth Week

Monday	Gal 4:22—5:1
Tuesday	Gal 5:1–6
Wednesday	Gal 5:18–25
Thursday	Eph 1:3–10
Friday	Eph 1:11–14
Saturday	Eph 1:1, 5–23

Twenty-Ninth Week

Monday	Eph 2:1–10
Tuesday	Eph 2:12–22
Wednesday	Eph 3:2–12
Thursday	Eph 3:14–21
Friday	Eph 4:1–6
Saturday	Eph 4:7–16

Thirtieth Week

Monday	Eph 4:32—5:8
Tuesday	Eph 5:21–33
Wednesday	Eph 6:1–9
Thursday	Eph 6:10–20
Friday	Phil 1:1–11
Saturday	Phil 1:18–26

Thirty-First Week

Monday	Phil 2:1–4
Tuesday	Phil 2:5–11
Wednesday	Phil 2:12–18
Thursday	Phil 3:3–8
Friday	Phil 3:7—4:1
Saturday	Phil 4:10–19

Thirty-Second Week

Monday	Ti 1:1–9
Tuesday	Ti 2:1–8, 11–14
Wednesday	Ti 3:1–7
Thursday	Phlm 7–20
Friday	2 Jn 4–9
Saturday	3 Jn 5–8

Thirty-Third Week

Monday	Rv 1:1–4; 2:1–5
Tuesday	Rv 3:1–6; 14–22
Wednesday	Rv 4:1–11
Thursday	Rv 5:1–10
Friday	Rv 10:8–11
Saturday	Rv 11:4–12

Thirty-Fourth Week

Monday	Rv 14:1–5
Tuesday	Rv 14:14–19
Wednesday	Rv 15:1–4
Thursday	Rv 18:21–23; 19:1–3, 9
Friday	Rv 20:1–4, 11–21
Saturday	Rv 22:1–7

Key to Abbreviations of Books of Scripture

Acts	Acts	2 Kgs	2 Kings
Am	Amos	Lam	Lamentations
Bar	Baruch	Lk	Luke
1 Chr	1 Chronicles	Lv	Leviticus
2 Chr	2 Chronicles	Mal	Malachi
Col	Colossians	1 Mc	1 Maccabees
1 Cor	1 Corinthians	2 Mc	2 Maccabees
2 Cor	2 Corinthians	Mi	Micah
Dn	Daniel	Mk	Mark
Dt	Deuteronomy	Mt	Matthew
Eccl	Ecclesiastes	Na	Nahum
Eph	Ephesians	Neh	Nehemiah
Est	Esther	Nm	Numbers
Ex	Exodus	Ob	Obadiah
Ezr	Ezra	Phil	Philippians
Ez	Ezekiel	Phlm	Philemon
Gal	Galatians	Prv	Proverbs
Gn	Genesis	Ps	Psalms
Hb	Habakkuk	1 Pt	1 Peter
Heb	Hebrews	2 Pt	2 Peter
Hg	Haggai	Rev	Revelation
Hos	Hosea	Rom	Romans
Is	Isaiah	Ru	Ruth
Jas	James	1 Sm	1 Samuel
Jb	Job	2 Sm	2 Samuel
Jdt	Judith	Sg	Song of Songs
Jer	Jeremiah	Sir	Sirach
Jgs	Judges	Tb	Tobit
Jl	Joel	1 Thes	1 Thessalonians
Jn	John	2 Thes	2 Thessalonians
1 Jn	1 John	Ti	Titus
2 Jn	2 John	1 Tim	1 Timothy
3 Jn	3 John	2 Tim	2 Timothy
Jon	Jonah	Wis	Wisdom
Jos	Joshua	Zec	Zechariah
1 Kgs	1 Kings	Zep	Zephaniah